A CITIZEN'S 2% SOLUTION

A CITIZEN'S 2% SOLUTION

How To
Repeal Investment Income Taxes,
Avoid a Value-Added Tax,
And Still Balance the Budget

S. DOUGLAS HOPKINS

A
Citizen's
Press

A Citizen's 2% Solution:
How to Repeal Investment Income Taxes, Avoid a Value-Added Tax, and
still Balance the Budget
First Edition
ISBN [978-0-9828328-0-6]
Ebook ISBN [978-0-9828328-1-3]

Published by:
A Citizen's Press, LLC
P.O. Box 82
Sparta, NJ 07871-0082
www.acitizenspress.com

cover design by Robert Aulicino

Dedication

*To my sons
Calvin and Clayton
and to Their Future Children
and Their Children's Children*

With Hope and Optimism

*With Love, Thanks and Appreciation
to my wife Angela
and to our respective parents
Monty, Brownie, Steve and Colleen
without all of whom I would not have such*

Hope and Optimism

CONTENTS

PROLOGUE

WHAT'S WRONG WITH THIS PICTURE?

In 2004 the *Wall Street Journal* published an editorial which included the following chart comparing information extracted from Teresa Heinz Kerry's 2003 tax return to 2001 tax information for the overall public showing that Ms. Heinz-Kerry paid a lower tax rate than the average paid by all U.S. taxpayers in 2001.

Wealth and Loopholes- Average federal income tax rate	
Teresa Heinz Kerry, 2003	**12.4 %**
All Taxpayers, 2001	14.2
Top 1%, 2001	27.5
Top 10%, 2001	21.4
Top 25%, 2001	18.1
Top 50%, 2001	15.9
Sources: Kerry Campaign, Tax Foundation	

The text of the editorial went on to provide some additional detail, revealing that the primary driver of her low effective tax rate was the fact that over half of Ms. Heinz-Kerry's gross income of $5.07 million came from tax exempt investments in state, municipal and public entity bonds. She paid $627,000 in taxes on taxable income of $2.29 million.

The Wall Street Journal's ("WSJ") focus with their editorial was upon the fact that her husband, Senator John Kerry, was at that time advocating an increase in the top marginal federal income tax rate from 35% to 39.6% to apply to all earners with income over $200,000, implying it was a tax which would be assessed upon the rich (and only the rich). The WSJ's conclusion was that the mega-millionaires like Mr. Kerry's wife would be able to continue investing in tax advantaged options, thus avoiding the new tax, while the working upper-middle class would be the bearers of the increased taxes.

They pointed out that according to the IRS, the Top 50% of all federal filers contributed 96.1% of all federal income taxes, and at 15.9%, that was 3.5 percentage points, or 22% higher than Ms. Heinz-Kerry's tax rate. They ended the editorial with the following summary conclusion:

> "At the very least, Mrs. Kerry's tax returns are a screaming illustration of the need for reform to make the tax code simpler and fairer. But they also show that Senator Kerry's proposed tax increases are much more about a revenue grab than they are about tax justice."

I shared some of the WSJ's concern and observations about the lack of equity inherent in the tax code as revealed by the disclosures in question. But it was another matter which really drew my attention.

Buried in the midst of the article was the observation that her $5.07 million income was "hardly surprising for someone estimated to be worth nearly $1 billion". My question was, how could she be so financially incompetent as to be earning only a 0.5% return on her assets? Even assuming her estimated net worth was over-stated by 30%, income of $5 million represented less than ¾ percent on her net worth. By my rough calculations, Ms. Heinz-Kerry paid somewhere in the range of 0.06% to 0.09% of her net worth in federal taxes in 2003. That's 6/100 to 9/100 of one percent.

Now, it so happened that 2003 was a very good year for me personally. By Wall Street standards it wouldn't have turned heads, but I considered it an exceptional year. I took advantage of the mortgage interest deduction and the full opportunity available to me to make tax-free contributions to my retirement plans and still paid an effective federal tax rate of 25.1%. I was happy to be in the position where I had earned as much as I did, and, as much as anyone's ever "happy" about paying taxes, when my wife and I filed our joint return we were content to contribute our part.

However, reexamining things in relationship to the disclosures from the Kerry's I became a little less sanguine.

In real terms, my wife and I paid a little less than 30% as much as Ms. Heinz-Kerry paid in federal taxes although our income was only about 15% as high. Our effective tax rate was thus roughly twice as high the Kerrys', which I confess I felt to be somewhat less than fully equitable. Worse yet, when I set out to examine the relationship between our tax burden and net worth I discovered that we were **paying roughly 100 times as high a tax rate** as Ms. Heinz-Kerry. In 2003 our federal taxes equaled 8.3% of my gross net worth, including tax deferred saving accounts.

> *"The story is always the same: Higher rates are imposed and at the same time loopholes are carefully framed which permit the wealthy to get out from under the higher rates."*
> — Hubert H. Humphrey (1911-1978)

Is the Heinz-Kerry tax situation unique? Not at all.

In October of 2007 Warren Buffet issued a challenge promising to donate $1 million to the favorite charity of any member of the Forbes 400 list of wealthiest Americans who can successfully refute Buffett's assertion that they (each and every Forbes 400 Member) paid an average tax rate that was lower than that paid by his or her receptionist.

Buffett, himself a member of the Forbes 400, says he prepares his own taxes without an accountant, does not use tax shelters, and paid only 17.7% of his income in taxes on his approximate $46 million income in the prior year. He further reported that the average tax rate for his office staff was 32.9% and none of his employees paid a rate as low as his own.

To date, no one has stepped forward to collect on Mr. Buffett's bet.

"Progress is impossible without change, and those who cannot change their minds cannot change anything."
— George Bernard Shaw (1856-1950)

PREFACE

I would like to start off with a respectful request of the reader. Please keep an open mind.

It is fairly unusual for an adult to set aside deeply or long-held beliefs and change their world view in a significant manner. It is quite difficult. By our nature, we tend to sort new facts into our pre-existing view of the world. I am often astounded by how remarkably adept we can be at totally discarding facts which don't fit our pre-existing view, or alternatively, maintaining multiple simultaneous beliefs and convictions which are in such direct conflict as to be mutually exclusive. But changing one's view is possible. I know. I've done it. I'm fifty-six years old and have long been a laissez-faire capitalist with a belief that lower marginal tax rates, particularly on investments, encourage and stimulate a vibrant and growing economy. I still believe that. Yet here I am, not only proposing a new tax, but a tax assessed directly upon accumulated wealth. (I hope I didn't spoil it for you, but I presumed that by the time anyone actually purchased this book they would have peeked ahead to obtain some idea of what was to come.)

It is my hope that the audience for this topic will not be restricted simply to people predisposed toward my conclusion. If it is, it will not serve its purpose. Its purpose and intent is to stimulate an open and broad-ranging dialogue regarding a topic of great importance which is, unfortunately, too often restricted and guided by myopic thinking, misplaced pragmatism, and provincial self-interest. My target for that discussion is not just tax policy, but the fundamental workings of democracy in the United States of America.

I describe this book as my proposal for "Rational and Equitable Tax Reform". "Rational and Equitable." Both highly subjective terms, perhaps even an invitation to argument. If I describe my view as being rational and equitable, and you disagree with it, you will quite likely find my description incendiary. I apologize

13

for that. I use the words rational and equitable to describe my objectives. I may not have achieved them. But if you can keep an open mind to both my attempt at "factual" observations and my conclusions, you might find yourself drawn into some thoughtful rumination on the topic.

If I have come to a flawed conclusion, perhaps some more insightful and open-minded reader might be stimulated to formulate an alternate proposal which does achieve my goal of "Rational and Equitable Tax Reform".

* * *

Author's Perspective:

All of us view the world through biased lenses, colored by the direct and indirect influences of our life: family, teachers, peers, mentors, adversaries, cultural background, financial situation, and other interactions with life and society experienced through both chance and choice.

In an ideal world, one might expect that a writer or speaker could and should be evaluated strictly upon his or her words and concepts. Indeed there are people who might argue that important and challenging concepts should be evaluated in a vacuum, shielded from knowledge of the source – thereby limiting subconscious ingrained biases of the listener.

However, I personally ascribe more validity to the counter argument. It can be very helpful to have a bit of knowledge about a speaker's background. It is in that spirit that I offer a bit of insight into mine.

I am not an Ivy League graduate and the views set forth hereafter have not been shaped by an economics mentor or intense academic study. I do of course read, research and explore other opinions about ideas and questions of interest to me, but the ideas set forth in this book emanate more from my life experience than from any existing academic theory or influence of which I am aware. There are probably some people who will find this factor alone reason enough to discard this book and consideration of the observations and conclusions discussed within it. I hope you will restrain that urge. I believe my lack of insulation and privilege is part of what gives me a perspective fresh enough to be worth sharing. (Note: I won't be offended if you want to skip forward here, but if you value perspective, be patient. I won't spend more than a couple pages on this and will move on to the point in short order.)

My parents met in high school in a very small farming community in central Ohio. I remember five of my great grandparents clearly and knew all four of my grandparents very well. I spent all my early summers and vacations on the farm, learning how to work hard by example and necessity. In my early youth, I had ambitions of someday taking over my grandfather's farm. I grew out of it. I was surrounded by three generations of hard-working, well-read, highly-opinionated mid-westerners who were actively engaged in pursuing the American Dream. For most of the younger generations, that meant a life away from the farm, working with their brains instead of their backs.

A recent family gathering was attended by nearly a dozen teachers, spanning grade school to graduate school, a retired federal judge, several writers, and a smattering of business execs, current and former military personnel, local and federal government administrators, as well as entrepreneurs, craftsmen, tradesmen, and farmers. The only particularly unusual observations I might make about the crowd was that it included a rather high incidence of ex-Peace Corps volunteers and other world travelers than might be normal and had experienced a notably low divorce rate – issues I find fascinating, but from which I draw no conclusions.

Early in my adult life I was a happily struggling actor, singer and screenwriter. During the course of a dozen years spent pursuing those high-risk, high-reward activities, I also held jobs as a laborer, fork-lift operator, bus-boy, bartender, taxi driver, waiter, actuarial accountant, office assistant, data processing clerk, internal auditor, camera grip, lighting assistant, script reader and story editor. Eventually, an opportunity which arose from an intermittent but recurring part-time position in accounting and financial analysis intersected with the desire to have a wife and family and led me to a career in management consulting.

For over twenty-five years now I have provided consulting services in the form of advisory assistance and/or interim management to financially stressed businesses. I found that the turnaround consulting field fit my personality quite well. Intellectually challenging and never dull, it is crisis driven, following a counter-cyclical boom and bust pattern. Over the past two and a half decades it has exposed me to a very diverse set of problem solving challenges. I have personally worked on nearly 100 different troubled company assignments to businesses with values ranging from $20 million to roughly $2 billion.

The core competency of my consulting practice is a disciplined, fact-intensive problem diagnosis process. In 2006, I co-authored *"Crafting Solutions for Troubled Businesses"*, published by BeardBooks, which describes that process as an approach to confronting management challenges. One of my reasons for writing this book is my perception that the issues and challenges I am deeply concerned about so seldom receive much disciplined factual analysis.

For most of my life I have been studiously apolitical. As noted, I grew up among a diverse crowd of argumentative and opinionated people. They debated and argued over everything. But I wasn't very old before I noticed that politics and religion tended to be the two topics which consistently generated the most heat and the least light. As a result, when I reached the age where I became a participant in these arguments, I found myself avoiding religion entirely (for fear of stimulating someone's premature heart attack) and treating politics as entertainment. I knew that little I said was likely to change anyone's opinion, but I took great pleasure in setting off the fireworks, whether I truly held legitimate differences of opinion or was just playing Devil's Advocate. Political debates were entertaining intellectual exercise, but I had no illusions that anything I thought might have any influence upon actual policy.

However, over the past ten years or so I have found my perspective changing. Whether it's just the premature onset of grumpy old age or a response to real deterioration in the public political dialogue, politics has begun to lose its entertainment value for me. I've begun to perceive the issues as too important to simply shrug off and laugh at. Certainly, much that occurs in the political landscape is still laughable. But it's not funny. Perhaps it's the influence of having children, two now-teenage boys.

I have voted in every election since I came of age, but I haven't done it with too much enthusiasm or sense of meaningful participation. One out of three eligible Americans are so disenfranchised they don't bother to vote at all. The fringe constituencies drive policy and the voting districts are heavily weighted in favor of the incumbents. The voting choices are very narrow. Which elite do you want to be governed by? Which candidate will do the least damage? Who's got the most trustworthy smile?

Left to their own devices, we cannot rely upon our political class to change the course of the nation. Someone has to change the dialogue and focus. In this book I am not just playing the Devil's Advocate. This book is my attempt to stimulate and participate in a dialogue which I believe to be important to the future path of the nation and the welfare of my sons and all our future generations.

* * *

Acknowledgments and Thanks:

For reasons already illuminated in the prologue, I would like to thank Senator John Kerry and his wife Teresa Heinz-Kerry and Warren Buffett, none of whom I have had the pleasure or privilege of meeting personally, for the public statements and disclosures which provided the intellectual stimulus and jumping-off platform of questions and realizations which led to this book. I want to make it very clear that I do not mean to imply any personal criticism toward either the Kerry's or Mr. Buffett or to suggest there is anything inappropriate or unethical in them, or anyone else, availing themselves of the benefits provided by our tax code. I am most appreciative of the Heinz-Kerry's for disclosing, and the Wall Street Journal for publishing, the disclosures which set the wheels of my mind turning. I am likewise grateful to Warren Buffett for using the power of his position to further illuminate the breadth of the issue.

On a more personal note, I would like to thank my wife, Angela, for her exceptional patience as I have embarked on this time and attention consuming journey of civic evaluation, and my parents, Stephen and Colleen, who instilled in me during my formative years the curiosity, confidence and sense of civic duty which have driven me to do so. In addition, my father, who has also been my long-term business partner and my co-author in our previous book, has provided invaluable assistance as a sounding board relative to both the form and substance of this book. Without his support and encouragement I am sure I would still be chasing ideas around on assorted scraps of paper and pursuing them over dinner conversations rather than in this open invitation for a broad public dialogue and call for reform.

A Nod to Matt Miller

Simultaneously with sending this book out to the printer, I learned that I was inadvertently about to overlap the title of a 2003 book released by Matt Miller, *The Two Percent Solution: Fixing America's Problems in Ways Liberals and Conservatives Can Love.* I immediately rushed out to find a copy and determined that while our titles did overlap, his usage of the two percent reference has a notably different context than mine. After consideration, I chose not to modify my message by a major title change. I did modify my title slightly to minimize confusion between our books. My apologies to Mr. Miller if he finds any insult in the fact I proceeded with the overlap. None was intended.

In fact, having now read it, *I highly recommend his book.* While my book is primarily focused upon a potential solution to revenue challenges and the inadequacies and inequities of tax policy, i.e. *how we can modify tax policies* in order to pay for important government programs, Mr. Miller's takes a different approach, focused on specific policy failures and political deadlocks, the issue of *why we need and should be willing to increase taxes.*

While Mr. Miller espouses a "big picture" activist role for government toward which I am skeptical, it is thoughtfully presented and I believe we hold and express very compatible and complementary views upon the need for change in the political process and tenor of policy debate.

And finally, a warm and enthusiastic thank you to Nina Novak, who supplied encouragement and insightful questions and generously shared resources as she guided me through the mysterious book production and distribution process. Her discerning and meticulous eye for detail eliminated countless errors and inconsistencies which would otherwise have appeared as distractions on the printed page.

PART I

WORTHY ASPIRATIONS

"What we face is above all a moral issue. At stake are not just the details of policy, but fundamental principles of social justice and the character of the country."
— Ted Kennedy, (1932-2009) in a letter to President Obama quoted in a 9/9/09 address to a joint session of Congress.

"The character of our country?....   One of the unique and wonderful things about America has always been our self-reliance: our rugged individualism, our fierce defense of freedom, and our healthy skepticism of government."
— President Barack Obama, (1961-) 9/9/09 (same forum)

CHAPTER 1

LAND OF THE FREE,
HOME OF THE BRAVE

Is there a *National Character of America*?

Over the labor day weekend which preceded President Obama's comments quoted above, at an extended family gathering attended by four generations of highly independent and opinionated Hopkins' (plus spouses, friends and partners), conversation turned to politics and economics, topics of sufficient interest, importance and controversy to ensure spirited disagreement and debate. However, there was one topic which was greeted with surprising unanimity. On several occasions, in discussing political challenges I happened to use the words "equitable" and "fair". On every occasion when I did so, I got hooted down. The one point of agreement among the crowd was that there was no room in American politics for equitable or fair. I didn't dare go so far as to speak of social justice.

I grew up believing that America was the *Best Country in the World*.

Actually that's not accurate. What I was taught and learned was far more specific and positive. America was presented as the *Land of Opportunity* – a land and country developed in such a way that it had a unique set of characteristics that set it apart from much of the rest of the world. Certainly I believed it was the best place on earth. But it was not a sense of braggadocio that made it best, it was respect and pride for the underlying qualities and character of the nation. It was a land where anything was possible – to anyone.

Although many Americans today seem to have missed or misinterpreted it, the lesson I remember being continuously drummed into my head in my youth was the importance of character. Character not just in the descriptive sense, the "aggregate of features and traits that form the individual nature of some person or thing", but in a broader, morally up-lifting sense I was taught that there was indeed a noble and defining character to our nation and I was challenged to live up to that standard.

Americans were brave and honest. They were just and truthful. They were proud and independent. They were self-sufficient and self-reliant, but still respected their fellow citizens' rights. They protected the weak.

"We the People"… Every schoolchild was taught the phrase. It imbues the core of the dream that is America. A joint mission. A community of equals, recognizing each to have "certain inalienable rights" setting forth principles of government intended to better the lives of all.

I still get chills just thinking about it.

Now before you pop a blood vessel or hurl this book across the room – don't get me wrong. I'm neither ignorant, nor naïve. I'm very much aware that the idealized version of our founding fathers did not exist in 1776. "We the People" did not include *Blacks*. And it did not include *Women*. The drafters of those words, as well as the Constitution yet to come, were privileged, land-owning *White Men* – slave-owners included.

Yet somehow they not only defined an ideal well worth striving for, they designed a structure of government which has allowed the United States to evolve, however slowly and uncertainly, toward their targeted goal of "a more perfect Union".

So back to my opening question, "Is there a National Character?" I believe there is… and its roots emanate from that ideal set forth in the Declaration of Independence, an ideal grounded far more firmly in aspiration than in fact, "We the People". It was an ideal arrogantly and bravely established on self-contradictory principles: pride, independence, self-interest, and self-reliance, all mixed with a sense of community, responsibility, and duty – joint sacrifice for the common good.

Though it may be subject to massive and obvious factual contradictions and egregious shortcomings, for over two hundred years the American character has been central to our history and our culture. In our history and our fiction – a strong moral compass has been central to the depiction of the American character; integrity and self-sacrifice tempering an entrepreneurial drive toward progress and personal success.

What was the legacy of our first President? "I cannot tell a lie. I chopped down the cherry tree."

The words of Patrick Henry? "Give me liberty or give me death!"

Nathan Hale, "I regret I have but one life to give for my country."

Are these historical quotes literally accurate, or enhanced by broad dramatic license? It hardly matters. They are part of the American psyche. They are central to the American psyche.

Classic American fiction incorporates a similar, frequently recurring theme: "common" figures made heroic by their integrity and self-sacrifice in the service of a greater good. For example: Huck Finn, the most ignorant of the poor and under-privileged who is guided by his own conscience to set aside the bigotry of society and his times.

Of course this was not a uniquely American theme. Examples of the timeless appeal of this storyline, both historic and fictional, date back at least to 480 BC and the Spartan defense of Thermopylae. Perhaps the most romantic version of this tale of self-sacrifice was Charles Dickens' 1859 novel, *A Tale of Two Cities*, "It is a far better thing I do...etc".

But it is a theme that seems to have been universally embraced by America.

As a young boy growing up in the 50's and 60's it was ever-present in the classic Western mythology of integrity facing adversity on the frontier: the Sheriff in High Noon, facing down the bad guys alone on behalf of townspeople too frightened to stand behind him – simply because it needed to be done; Shane – the reluctant gunfighter – struggling to set aside his deadly past but compelled by his nature/conscience to protect those unable to protect themselves.

Once again the gap between fact and fiction was a vast chasm. The real west was brutal, violent and ambiguous. Jesse James was a cold-blooded killer who, based on most factual accounts, seems to have deserved the bullet in the back which brought him down.

But the mythology still resonated - and arguably made us better. The carryover of the theme may have blurred the lines between fact and fiction and distorted the reality of the times, but it created something worthy to emulate.

Even the treatment of the vanquished Indians seems uniquely American.

For centuries, all around the world, the expansion of empires has been a recurring story of conquest and subjugation. The winners rule the losers and write history to exalt their own righteous superiority – in which they emerge standing with their foot on the necks of their "inferiors".

In actuality the American Indians fared no better, indeed much worse, than most of the previously vanquished across the world. They were cheated and abused, driven from their lands, and substantially eradicated by the European explorers. Yet the American Indian was not subjugated by the invaders and ruled as inferior beings, as were the natives of colonies in Africa, India and Asia. The vanquished American Indians became mythologized as Noble Savages, despite the fact that their treatment, like that of the Black Africans imported as slaves, is a dark and bloody stain upon American History.

So how did this factually questionable "American Character" take hold of our imaginations and become ingrained in our self-image? Once again, I must cite the phrase "We the People". Despite their narrow interpretation of who the "People" were, in setting forth the intention to identify and acknowledge "inalienable rights" – and *protect them even against the majority* – the founders set America on a uniquely positive path. In my opinion the key to that path was the intermingling of pride and self-interest with responsibility and duty, and the form of representative government that emerged from that mixture.

The recognition and enumeration of individual rights, and the establishment of protections for those rights, is both the core element of the American Democracy and the defining driver of the American character.

The founders stood up as a group to overthrow the English King, shedding the yoke of servitude which they felt heavy upon their shoulders. But they did not do so in order to establish themselves as the new, privileged, ruling elite – they stepped forward to serve the common good, speaking and acting on behalf of their fellow citizens as well as themselves. Upon achieving success and ousting the British they did not immediately turn toward self-enrichment (at least not too egregiously) but they continued to develop the fledgling government in support of their inclusive ideals and the new society which they now led.

Many now seem to think that America's core value has always been laissez-faire Capitalism; a belief that the unfettered exercise of individual self-interest is the most efficient driver to economic progress and growth. But it was not exclusively personal self-interest that drove the founders or shaped the Union they formed. It was an abiding respect for universal, individual rights and rejection of hereditary wealth and power.

America was conceived as a land of equal opportunity. Not equality of circumstances, but a society where commoners need not defer to elites, and every man had an opportunity to better his position. The American Revolution was a grand experiment. It did not merely seek to supplant one set of elite rulers with another, but to change the fundamental organization of society. It disdained and rejected the concept of hereditary privilege while still elevating the goal of success. Unlike socialist regimes that were later to develop in other parts of the world, our fledgling American government was not designed to take from the rich so much as to allow an opportunity for the common man to rise and become rich. By 1835, in contrast to the aristocratic models which had dominated Europe for centuries, French political scientist Alexis de Tocqueville described America as a society where hard work and money-making was the dominant ethic. That new dominant ethic was not then, nor is it now, universally perceived as an improvement. But it was certainly a new direction, providing hope and encouragement to the masses.

America's government was not designed to support and protect the powerful, nor to bring them down to a common level, but rather to allow the entire citizenry the opportunity to rise. It protected not just citizens as a group, but citizens as individuals, against abuses of power. The scope of federal powers and authority was expressly limited. Its organization and structure provided for checks and balances against the inappropriate use of those powers. It was composed of citizen representatives, elected for limited terms to act on behalf of their constituents.

Participation in the government was not designed to facilitate the exercise of power by the privileged in pursuit of personal self-interest. Unlike the aristocratic models wherein powers of government either came as rights associated to holders of existing wealth or were granted accompanied by rights of property, wealth, and income, participation in the American Congress was conceived as a civic service, performed on behalf of one's fellow citizens. Congress' members were selected from within the communities of its States to serve and returned back to those communities when their service was completed.

Congress was conceived to be populated with true *Citizen Representatives*: Men (and only much later women) with active lives, careers, land-holdings, business-holdings, and family and community relationships who served as individuals dutifully, but temporarily, on behalf of their communities. It should not be underestimated how much establishing and maintaining this particular aspect of representative government was, and is, critical to the goals of the Union.

I believe that there is indeed a National Character of America, and that it was articulated in its Declaration of Independence and codified in its Constitution and Bill of Rights. It honors pride, independence and personal freedom, but joins with that a sense of responsibility and duty toward the common good. It acknowledges inalienable rights of the individual and aggressively protects them against the whims and prejudices of the majority. It values and rewards personal accomplishment, but disdains claims of hereditary superiority. It is a challenge, a duty and an honor that must be maintained and upheld by its *Citizen Representatives*.

Unfortunately, as at the inception of its Union, America's National Character continues to exist more perfectly in aspiration than in fact.

Still, it is an aspiration worthy of our continued active pursuit.

PART II

REALITY BITES

"I cannot tell a lie. It was I that chopped down the cherry tree."
— attributed by popular myth to young George Washington, (1732-1799) future first President of the United States of America.

"I want to say one thing to the American people. ... I did not have sexual relations with that woman..."
— President William Jefferson Clinton, (1946-   ) recorded wagging his finger at the camera lens while in office on January 26, 1998

CHAPTER 2

A NATION OF LIARS

Is there any doubt why the reputation of politicians has fallen so far since the establishment of the Union?

There may well be more than one reason. But a long-standing pattern of playing fast and loose with the truth certainly ranks high upon the list.

Numerous defenders of President Clinton were quick to point out that the issue in question when he made his infamous denial was personal in nature, not official business of his office and, therefore, neither the press nor public had any right to knowledge or explanation of the matter, true or false.

A smaller group asserted that he wasn't under oath and simply lying to the public wasn't a crime – or even a notably unique practice among politicians.

A still smaller group argued that his denial wasn't a lie – but was carefully, even skillfully, crafted to be defensible as accurate while still obscuring the "truth", similar to the circumlocutions with which he parsed the meaning of the word "is" while he was under oath. The implication of admiration for his skill in this matter was perhaps what irritated me most from Clinton's many defenders. Absent a political imperative for pretending otherwise, no rational person could fail to discern his statements as anything but a direct, deliberate, pre-meditated lie to the public which he served.

For what it's worth, in my opinion the use of political power and prestige to induce an intern assigned to the White House to engage in sexual acts (whether discernable from sexual "relations" or not) was a deplorable and embarrassing act which cheapened the office of President – but probably did not rise to the level of an impeachable offense. I am further reluctantly forced to admit that the practice of lying to the public is so commonplace by politicians of every level that I must agree with the assessment that his lie about his personal sexual peccadilloes did not rise to an impeachable offense either.

Nevertheless, I do think we ought to take a step back and ask a couple of questions. First, how did we make the journey from George Washington to Bill Clinton; from a President reputedly unable to tell a lie, to one who couldn't be expected not to? Second, what damage have we inflicted upon ourselves by doing so?

How can our leadership, both those directly holding political office and the chattering classes of media and influence that surround them, look themselves in the mirror every morning?

I suspect that it is simply because disdain for the truth has become endemic in our society. It is not a practice which is in any way restricted to political forums, but it is in the political arena that it has been raised to its highest art form. Swindlers and embezzlers have to lie well. Politicians merely have to move their lips.

Dismiss that as a joke if you can. I concede, it's a facile one-liner and I'm not the first to use it. But can you pretend it's not true? I can't anymore. The facts have become too compelling and I believe the loss of integrity in political discourse is the source of too much damage.

Bernie Madoff had to make people believe him. He had to be credible. He looked people in the eye and told them that he was going to "do good" and make them rich at the same time. He promised above market returns with below market risks – a classic something-for-nothing con. But he had to make it a good story. He had to work hard at it.

He rubbed shoulders with the rich and powerful. He worked the charitable functions and trusts and seeded the ground liberally with his own money. He sympathized with his clients' values and supported their priorities. He assembled enthusiastic, high profile, reputable figures to vouch for his authenticity – presumably most of them unwittingly. He provided documentary evidence, actual pieces of paper, to prove that he was as good as his word. He even went so far as to cite scrutiny received from the SEC as proof that his operations were squeaky clean. It's not easy to run a large Ponzi scheme for years without being called out for it. You have to be a very convincing liar.

The hurdle for politicians is much, much lower. They look us in the eye.... and tell us what we want to hear. So we disengage ourselves from reality and believe them.

They know they're lying. We know they're lying. They know we know they're lying. And I believe that anyone who says it isn't so – is lying.

> *"The American Republic will endure until the day Congress discovers that it can bribe the public with the public's money."*
> — Alexis de Tocqueville, (1805-1859) in Democracy in America, publ. 1835

Tocqueville was wrong. He underestimated the strength of the American Republic. It remains intact, long after Congress made that discovery. But he was prescient in his identification of the problem and the potential damage it would inflict. One doesn't have to be a deficit hawk to see that the damage is accelerating.

We, both the public and the press, are deeply complicit in the problem. We accept political lies as though they were inconsequential, even as they fill us with disgust and turn us off from the political process. It happens in multiple ways for multiple reasons.

First and foremost, of course, is Tocqueville's concern, bribery. Just like Bernie Madoff, our politicians promise us something for nothing. We know it's not true. We know it is fundamentally dishonest. We know that in order to give something to us they have to take it from someone else. But in a government where the political imperative is to "bring home the bacon", we also know that if we don't grab our share somebody else will. So we bemoan the fact that everybody else's representatives are crooks while we try to make sure that our representative will be the biggest pig at the trough.

That's the cynical view.

A more generous perspective credits our representatives with higher motives and forgives them for their pragmatic acceptance of a flawed and imperfect process. To do that, we have to rely upon that familiar and dangerous rationalization – that *the end justifies the means.*

However you choose to view it the underlying facts remain the same; honesty and integrity have been grotesquely devalued. In fact, they have become a serious political liability.

In a recent editorial published by *Newsweek*, journalist Robert Samuelson referred to the Orwellian nature of our political discourse and described the issue as well as anyone can, stating that, "Reconciling blatantly contradictory objectives requires them (the administration) to engage in willful self-deception, public dishonesty, or both". He's absolutely right, yet still manages to understate the problem. The deeper problem is that we have reached a point where the ability to engage in either self-deception or public dishonesty has become a requirement for holding high public office. Samuelson's observation was calmly and accurately stated – but the tone of his statement was as illuminating as the content. It was devoid of outrage. There was remarkably little accusation in it. It was a simple statement of observed fact. We accept that this is how our public servants act.

Samuelson happened to be talking about the Obama administration and health care. But I believe it could just as accurately describe the actions of every administration in my lifetime in relationship to dozens of different issues. Honesty, which should represent an absolute minimum requirement for public service, has become a detriment to a political career. We expect and require our politicians to lie.

Surely, even George Orwell would be shocked at how far we've come. In his 1949 novel, *1984*, he imagined a society where language was actively distorted in order to obscure reality and control the populace. He described a practice he called "double-think", through which the public was consciously manipulated and trained to hold contradictory ideas without question – essentially taught to accept lies without critical thinking or questioning. Does that sound familiar? I believe Orwell intended to be writing a cautionary satire about the damaging course society was embarked upon. I don't believe he intended it to be a blueprint for political development and success.

But the ease and comfort with which we discuss and accept the current practice of politicians and media "spinning" the facts to suit their policies suggests that, in some circles, Orwell's cautions were accepted more as suggestions than warnings.

Media coverage of politics treats it like sports entertainment, focusing on strategy, image, short-term competitive advantages; who's up, who's down, who's controlling the dialogue of the day and who's wandered off of the talking points – making winning or losing the issue as though content and policy were matters of no consequence. In the name of "balance", they actively solicit and cite conflicting facts and allegations in support of each side but are shy about challenging or assessing those facts. They spend far more time reporting on the effectiveness of the political campaigns and campaigners relative to polls and elections, than evaluating the merits of policy or accuracy of assertions.

As an aside, perhaps I should acknowledge that I have already heard criticism of my choice to lead this chapter with reference to W J Clinton's now famous denial. People whose opinions and judgment I respect have suggested that it may be too politically charged and inflammatory, implying either a political affiliation with and bias in favor of the Republicans or a personal animus toward Mr. Clinton on my part. I apologize if that is the perception. It truly is not the case. Neither of America's dominant political parties, or indeed any of its factional interests, has any great advantage over the other(s) relative to honest discourse. Nor is it my desire to single Mr. Clinton out for more public scorn than he has already invited and received. Frankly I can't imagine anything adding to the embarrassment and scrutiny he has already faced. If he hasn't been sufficiently shamed already nothing I could say here would change that even if that were my intent.

But I simply could not imagine another example which so easily and completely illustrated my point – and left so little room for "principled" rejection of the charges. Among my more liberal friends I was encouraged to cite George Bush and Dick Cheney's assertions regarding Weapons of Mass Destruction, or Sarah Palin's "Death Panels". But those, like most other available targets, simply invite a debate about the difference between a lie, an error, a conflicting interpretation, and an illustrative exaggeration – all the standard defenses – arguments which tend to bear greater or lesser weight depending upon one's underlying principles, philosophies, and objectives, and their relationship to the target at hand.

Clinton's assertion was almost unique in how factually indefensible it was. It is not its prurient interest which draws me to it, but the astounding result wherein a large contingent of the political class stepped forward with a straight face to support the right of a politician to tell bald-faced lies to the public – without even the minimal cover of being able to argue it was in the service of a "greater good".

The example was chosen not because of the importance of the lie, but rather because its crass and indefensible nature illustrates so clearly that we have evolved a system in which our political representatives have lost all respect for the truth. They are prepared to defend the indefensible.

In fairness, dishonesty in public discourse is not a particularly new problem. Among the political classes and intellectual elite there has long been a large and otherwise reputable contingent who believe and argue that dishonesty in the service of political goals is not a problem, but a prerogative and obligation of power.

> *"If anyone at all is to have the privilege of lying, the rulers of the State should be the persons: and they, in their dealings either with enemies or with their own citizens, may be allowed to lie for the public good."*
> — Plato (427-347 BC)

> *"For a long time I have not said what I believed nor do I ever believe what I say, and if indeed sometimes I do happen to tell the truth, I hide it among so many lies that it is hard to find."*
> — Machiavelli (1469-1527)

> *"A man is justified in lying to protect the honor*
> *of a woman or to promote public policy"*
> — Woodrow Wilson (1856-1924)

One could easily fill an entire book with such rationalizations.

To do so, however, is to willfully miss the point. The strength of American Democracy was grounded in reliance that our government was acting on our behalf and in our collective interests. It was the recognition that Plato was wrong and that citizens should not be subordinate to their government.

The great improvement in the design of the American Democracy over prior iterations was a government "of the people" – not some beneficent elite, but citizen representatives, equal to us in all ways. It is not possible to treat one's fellow citizens as equals and act on their behalf while you are distorting the facts upon which decisions are being based. Likewise, it is not possible to make sound decisions when surrounded by distorted facts. This is particularly true when politics is a profession – not a public service, a matter I will return to in a later chapter.

Pragmatic defenders of the status quo will surely claim that seeking to banish dishonesty from government is a futile aim – an attempt to repeal the laws of human nature. Once again, such objections seek to willfully miss the point.

There is not an American over the age of three who does not know that lying is wrong. Greater Good be damned. Dishonest discourse in matters of public policy is anathema to a viable Democracy. We cannot achieve the goals to which we aspire if we pragmatically accept and encourage a lesser result. We cannot formulate good policy on the back of dishonest debate and misrepresented facts.

We cannot expect our political representatives to always be right. But we must demand that they always be honest. It is true, some of them won't be. The laws of human nature cannot be repealed. But we must aspire to more than what we are currently receiving. We cannot accept and condone duplicity and misrepresentations. We cannot give a wink and a nod and be complicit in practices which are warping the fabric of our institutions. The institutions of our American Democracy were constructed with checks and balances and limits on power precisely because we cannot rely solely on the goodness of our fellow man.

When we accept and tacitly encourage dishonest public discourse as the basis of governmental decision-making we undermine those checks and balances and the institutions themselves.

Of course, much of what I view and describe as "dishonest discourse" is not as straight forward as either the cherry tree or intern quotes cited above. Because of that they are far more invidious and damaging.

*"The little bit of truth contained in many a lie
is what makes them so terrible."*
— Marie von Ebner-Eschenbach
(1830-1916)

*"There are three kinds of lies: lies, damned lies,
and statistics. "*
— Benjamin Disraeli (1804-1888)

"The cruelest lies are often told in silence."
— Robert Louis Stevenson (1850-1894)

Since it is my intention to set forth here a short treatise, rather than a four volume tome, I will restrict myself to commenting further on only two key examples where I believe a lack of honesty is undermining important debate and decision-making – but the examples are not unique, simply two of the most egregious examples of a broad structural problem.

HEALTH CARE

As I write this Congress is actively negotiating the largest expansion in government seen in at least a half century. They are initiating regulations affecting roughly 1/6th of the U.S. economy based upon an acrimonious debate in which both sides characterize the other as duplicitous and self-serving. Those mutual accusations may be the most honest thing they have to say about the topic.

Some of the most intense heat has surrounded Sarah Palin's characterization that the health care proposals would lead to the creation of "Death Panels". It is highly illustrative of what I define as dishonest discourse.

Depending upon the listener's point of view, the Death Panel accusation may be:

a)   a bald-faced lie and knowing misrepresentation,
b)   an honest and bold revelation of the liberals' secret agenda,
c)   an inflammatory, and hyperbolic extrapolation of potential implications from legislative proposals, indicative of deep fear and distrust of others' motives and intentions, or
d)   some other random point on the continuum between a and b.

Personally, I think it falls rather neatly under point c. It was not intended to advance or illuminate the discussion. It was clearly intended to be inflammatory and hyperbolic. But it was not totally disconnected from fact. Further, it reveals a deep distrust of underlying intentions of her Democratic colleagues and fear of the unspoken truth.

If cost control is a serious goal then some form of rationing will have to be applied. Rationing is applied today. If you can't afford to pay and you don't have insurance coverage your access to health care is restricted.

Unless we intend to embrace a new dictum establishing universal, unlimited health care as a new human right, i.e. that everything that can be done will be done, and the government will guarantee payment for those services, services will continue to be rationed and care that may be desired will not always be available.

To date, I have not heard any serious politician step forward and directly advocate on behalf of that broad decree. This is not to say that there is no one advocating that health care should be a citizen's right. But I certainly have not heard anyone step forward to initiate honest debate about the very challenging trade-offs between what we can do, what we want to do, what we should do, and what we can afford to do.

Back to Ms. Palin's inflammatory assertion[1]. The Democratic proposals as currently set forward call for Congressionally mandated oversight panels to evaluate best practices in an effort to improve medical care and make it more cost effective. Clearly no one should be expected to believe that treatments and practices that are determined to be ineffective are going to be approved for continuation. It does not require a very large leap of imagination to infer that a panel charged with opining upon best practices will be advising that certain forms of care and treatment be reduced and restricted. Overlapping the common knowledge that a) resources are limited and b) cost effectiveness is one of the key criteria established to be considered by the panel's review, it is logical to assume that high cost procedures with statistically poor outcomes will be discouraged. Ergo: Death Panels.

An important question with regard to this line of reasoning and response in my view is whether it emanates from real underlying fear of the unknown, in which case a more honest dialogue might be productive in alleviating the rage, or some deep-seated antipathy toward and disrespect for any and everyone who views the world from a different perspective. Probably a bit of both.

In either event, it may be protected free speech, but the clowns who claim that "Obama wants to Kill Granny!" are engaging in highly dishonest discourse.

---

[1] The Death Panel language is popularly attributed to Ms. Palin and associated with a posting on her public web page, however, I have seen multiple references suggesting it was not actually original to Ms. Palin but had been previously published through other sources. It is not my intention to insult anyone by referring to it here in a manner consistent with the popular attribution.

On the other hand, so are the drafters of legislation who pretend that we can massively expand the reach and coverage of health services without either increasing costs or reducing services. Central to their cost control arguments are that they believe a) implementing evidence based best practices will lead to massive cost reductions in the delivery of health care services and/or b) as long as you characterize increased costs as being borne by someone else, they don't count.

An Aside:

Within weeks of the Death Panel assertion, which was aggressively charged by the administration to be totally and completely false, reckless and incendiary, in late October 2009 a highly qualified and presumably reputable review board issued public findings which reduced recommended guidelines for utilizing both mammograms and pap smears as cancer screening tools. In the case of mammograms it recommended that annual screenings commence after the age of 50 versus the existing practice of age 40. It was asserted that both revised recommendations were initiated without consideration of cost control concerns but solely based upon the scientific evidence and medical efficacy of the tests.

An immediate uproar ensued. Both the American Medical Association and American Cancer Society challenged the recommendations. The Republicans held them up as evidence of step one of government rationing citing (accurately) that such recommendations are generally utilized as critical components in the determination of what procedures insurance will cover. The Administration and its Congressional majority vehemently denied that it was their intention to utilize such recommendations to interfere with doctor/patient decisions about medical care.

Liars all. Either you use evidence based analysis of treatment efficacy to guide and control medical practices or you obtain no cost controls.

The U.S. Preventative Services Task Force, authors of the revised recommendations, quickly back-tracked, and insisted they weren't saying don't get an annual mammogram between 40 and 50 – just not recommending you should. They insisted that their intent was to leave the decision to each patient and their doctor. They apologized that they had communicated their findings poorly and explained that they were simply suggesting that, absent hereditary or other increased risk indicators, in their opinion, the benefits of annual screening between the ages of 40 and 50 might not outweigh the risks.

The benefit they cited was one life saved for every 1902 women screened. The risks, which they were reluctant to illuminate, included stress (related to false positives) and the unnecessary biopsies and other procedures related to treating non-lethal tumors identified by the screenings. If some counterbalancing number of deaths resulted from those unnecessary procedures I did not see it reported. I have no idea what the cost of 19,020 mammograms (1902 women screened in each of the ten years), plus associated "unnecessary" procedures might be. Again, I did not see it in any of the news reports regarding the panel's findings.

For the record, by my math, a very, very rough estimate of the annual lives saved comes to 1,026 women per year[2].

If my wife isn't already over fifty (I think it wise not to disclose this particular piece of data) I don't think she will be easily convinced that she should forgo annual mammograms – at least based upon the evidence cited publicly so far.

It is not my intention in citing this health care debate to try to suggest a viable policy, but simply to point out that the semantic dishonesty which riddles the conversation undermines realistic hopes for achieving effective reform.

It starts with the very basics. If we want to mandate universal coverage, and eliminate risk based pricing, then we are no longer talking about an insurance product but a social policy. If we want to convert from insurance based programs to mandatory risk pooling consortiums, and perhaps we should, then we should recognize that that is what we are setting forth to do and carefully examine the requirements and potential repercussions of those changes. We should stop the farce of pretending we are dealing with insurance reform and get on about the business of evaluating the delivery of health services. It would greatly facilitate the discussion.

We cannot make sound policy decisions if we can't, or won't, clearly acknowledge the underlying facts and the implications of our choices.

The Republicans are currently obstructing an important national policy discussion in the interests of regaining political advantage. The Democrats are engaging in knowing misrepresentations and factual distortions in an effort to ram through their long held ideal of universal coverage before their own political

---

[2] U.S. Population of 303.9M X 52.5% women ÷ 1902 (lives not saved by screening) ÷ 81.4 average female life expectancy. Data source: The Economist' Pocket World in Figures – 2010 Edition.

influence wanes – with little caution regarding the form it takes, how much it costs, or who pays for it[3].

I believe in fact-based decision making and am incensed that our leadership is so factionally split and integrity-challenged that they cannot lead an honest debate about the important and very difficult decisions that need to be addressed.

I suggest we all roll down our windows, stick our heads out, and shout in unison a quote from a fictional Italian poet and hot-head, "A Pox on Both Their Houses!"

Social Security

Social Security has long been acknowledged as the "Third Rail" of American politics: touch it and die. It has earned that name by virtue of the deep divide between what it is and was designed to be, and what the general public believes it is and demands from it.

Whether caused by gross and deliberate deceptions or actively encouraged misconceptions, the lack of understanding among the public that exists related to Social Security is a serious obstacle to changing what is almost universally agreed to be a pending financial debacle.

As its name implies, Social Security was conceived as a social program. It predates the current trend of disconnecting the content of a bill from its title. In the vernacular, it is a "safety net", designed to protect the aged poor from poverty following their retirement from the workforce. But it was sold to the public as a retirement savings program.

Social Security is not a retirement savings program. Payroll taxes withheld today are not the source of future withdrawals. There is no "lock box". The surplus Social Security funds collected from the population to date are an accounting entry. They are not segregated. They are not held in escrow. They have not been invested in physical or financial assets. They have been used to fund government operations. In return, the government has promised to pay certain future benefits, so long as they continue to operate the program. Understand clearly: the government has not provided individual contributors with any contractually enforceable promise regarding those future benefits. If they were to distill the existing governmental promise into writing it would include the words, "terms and conditions are subject to change at any time at the sole discretion of the government".

---

[3] The preceding was drafted prior to passage of the recent health care bill – but it didn't seem necessary to change the tense before publication because both party's actions in this regard continue unabated.

Still, massive public pressure exists to obstruct any modifications which might improve the program's long-term solvency and refocus it upon its intended goals and design.

Until and unless our political leaders are prepared to speak frankly and honestly, reeducate the public on the underlying goals and structure of the Social Security program, and disappoint a large portion of their constituents by acknowledging that we will have to reduce benefits paid to the well-off, raise the age at which one can draw benefits, and/or uncap the contribution limit, we will continue to stumble toward a financial train wreck.

I will say it again. Social Security is not a retirement savings plan. Social Security is not self-funding. If it were, the contributions would be escrowed and invested. Current Social Security contributions are being used to fund general government disbursements, including unsustainable deficits. As the population ages and current disbursements start to exceed current contributions, the difference will have to be funded either from general revenues or increased contributions.

You judge for yourself whether the references to a Social Security "lock box" or an "accumulated surplus" are intended to be misleading. But as a point of fact, the accumulated surplus is not held in the form of tangible assets. It is simply an accounting entry showing the quantity of funds which have been used by the government for other purposes. It represents an unsecured promise by the government to repay those funds. The sources from which it may do so are either future tax revenues or future borrowings.

Personally I believe they are misleading and that the public understanding of the facts and implications is quite low. However, I cannot opine as to whether that represents disregard for clarity, deliberate deception, or self-deception and a lack of financial acumen on the part of the speaker(s). Here again, I believe all of these factors come into play to greater and lesser degrees depending upon both the speakers and the audience.

> *"Nothing is as easy as deceiving yourself, for what you wish you readily believe."*
> — Demosthenes (384-322 BC)

It would not be difficult to continue citing other examples of such overt and covert political dishonesty, but hopefully the point is already clear. Key policy issues and choices are being obscured, sometimes willfully, sometimes perhaps inadvertently, by careless and irresponsible semantic and factual misrepresentations.

I have frequently observed in my business consulting practice that those companies which habitually construct their reporting to put a positive spin upon their actions and accomplishments find themselves at a deep disadvantage to those which utilize a more balanced factual presentation. When was the last time you watched a political debate when it didn't appear that the two parties had each brought their own divergent set of facts?

I will repeat an earlier observation – good decision making cannot rely upon distorted facts.

"It could probably be shown by facts and figures that there is no distinctly native American criminal class except Congress."

— Mark Twain (1835-1910)

"But shucks, we got the best politicians in this country that money can buy."

— Will Rogers (1879-1935)

"Anyone who is willing to undertake what is required to get elected to national public office is displaying a deep character flaw which ought to disqualify them from serving."

— unattributed[4]

---

[4] A longstanding, oft-offered axiom of the Author. I make no claims to its originality. If any reader can cite and provide proper attribution the Author would be happy to both learn the source and offer appropriate mea culpas for failure to cite same.

CHAPTER 3

THE CURSE OF PROFESSIONAL POLITICIANS

I recently formulated my own personal Magic Lamp List. I suspect that we have all at some time or another toyed with the three wishes question. It presents the challenge of examining and assessing values and priorities. If taken seriously it can sometimes become quite difficult to make a decision.

As we progress I will illuminate my full list, but for now I will simply say that item number one was a remarkably easy choice for me.

Wish #1. Banish Professional Politicians

If "Money is the Root of All Evil", and "Power Corrupts", why should it be surprising that professional politicians don't act like the Citizen Representatives that were anticipated by the founders upon the establishment of the Union? When a man, or woman, chooses to make politics their career, they take up residence at the intersection between money and power.

There are people who believe that the skills required to become a successful politician cannot be learned – that good politicians are born, not made. I feel that view is far too cynical. I hope that view is far too cynical. I believe the vast majority of our political class was drawn to the field with a genuine sense of purpose, a desire to contribute to society.

I don't believe that they were all born with that character flaw I referred to earlier. I believe the system we force them to work in creates it. I don't deny that I wish to stomp it out but I have deep sympathy for where it comes from.

How might it impact *your* character if you were to spend well over half your time begging for money, lots and lots of money – insane and unjustifiable sums of money, while carefully, subtly or not too subtly, reshaping your words and world-view to fit the conflicting requirements of your party machine, its donors and the universe of potential voters? All under the scrutiny of a media that seems more interested in the game of *Gotcha!* than reporting on issues of substance: a media *and public* which values controversy and photogenics far more highly than measured thought and judgmental nuance.

I don't like those job specifications. Do you? I can't pretend that if I subjected myself to that for any extended period of time it might not warp my character. Can you? And it doesn't even pay well, unless you bend to the siren call of graft that whispers in the corners and echoes off the walls.

The hallways and waiting rooms leading to the corridors of power are filled with money and temptation. We shove our politicians into those corridors and they are surrounded by money. Except for the grunts and go-fers, almost everyone they come in daily contact with reeks of money – even before you get to the big-money donor community. The advisors, pollsters, consultants and media support teams generally make more than the politicians they serve. The lobbyists make lots more.

The serious donors, the high-rollers whose help and support politicians crave and require, are typically not only outrageously successful and well-heeled; many are powerful and charismatic as well. They all are demanding.

I don't think this is the way the founders expected or intended the system to work.

Considering how the system does work I find it astounding, and an exemplary testament to the character and intentions of the vast majority of our elected officials, how little direct theft or graft there is in our government. Certainly, human nature being what it is, there are occasional instances where an elected official will be found with large sums of cash stashed in his freezer or under his mattress, siphoned out of the vast money flow and set aside for personal use. But in my opinion those instances of personal theft are surprisingly infrequent.

Unlike many other nations, where graft among the ruling classes takes the form of direct bribes and wire transfers to numbered bank accounts, in the upper echelons of American Congressional and Executive government most of the influence peddling is conducted in a less obvious form; it is a clubbier exercise of mutual back-scratching and common interests.

Look at the recent high-profile outrage in Chicago, where Illinois Governor Rod Blagojevich was impeached for attempting to sell President Obama's vacated Senate post. To my knowledge it has not yet been demonstrated that Blagojevich was seeking to directly line his personal pockets, but it is apparently undeniable that he was openly and aggressively attempting to obtain campaign contributions, fundraising commitments and/or other forms of favors and influence in return for the "prize" of a Senate appointment. As of this writing Blagojevich remains unapologetic, insisting he was doing nothing more than engaging in political horse-trading, like every other politician. It may be distasteful that he does it out in the open – but he has a point. How different was it from the day to day workings of the greater political machine?

I'm certainly not an apologist for Mr. Blagojevich, but was his attempt at ensuring that his favored appointee would "appreciate" the Senatorial assignment more or less despicable than Harry Reid granting the state of Nebraska perpetual immunity from increased Medicare enrollment costs in return for Senator Ben Nelson's vote to shut down further debate on the highly partisan and publicly unpopular health care bill?

Who, outside of government, would have dared to contemplate publicly engaging in such an outright and outrageous bribe? How does one justify outrage against Mr. Blagojevich's actions and then turn around and participate or acquiesce in Senator Reid's?

> *"It is as bad as going to Congress; none comes back innocent."*
> — Ralph Waldo Emerson (1803-1882)

The vast money flows, non-stop campaigns and obsequious fundraising our politicians become immersed in tend to warp their character and judgment. Far fewer give in to that siren call of outright graft than might reasonably be expected to. But they sever most connections with the real world and are molded by forces that distort their view and understanding of the reality of their fellow citizens' lives.

Modestly paid personally, they become rich in power. They are elevated to a rarified, ego-inflating, hubris-inducing upper strata of society where they are surrounded by so much Machiavellian intrigue, extravagance, and waste that they seem to lose all sense of the real value of things, particularly with regard to honesty and money.

The joke used to be that a Congressman was someone who didn't know the difference between a million and a billion. It's recently been inflated to the difference between a billion and a trillion. And the humor in that is distressingly hollow.

How can we send our citizens to Congress under these terms and expect them to act rationally on our collective behalf? We have developed a system that chooses them not for their virtue and wisdom but based upon how adept they are at seizing and holding power.

*"If ever this free people – if this Government itself is ever utterly demoralized, **it will come from this human wriggle and struggle for office** – a way to live without work; from which nature I am not free myself."*

— Abraham Lincoln (1809-1865)

"Anything is moral that furthers the main concern of his [the politician's] soul, which is to keep a place at the public trough."

— H L Mencken (1880-1956)

Few people had the talent for combining powers of acute observation with cynicism as effectively as Mencken, but you don't need to share his cynicism to see the underlying truth in his observation. When politics becomes a man's profession, of necessity, his primary incentive is to further that career. Elective positions are neither obtained nor defended by conducting good government, but by winning elections. A politician cannot accomplish anything without first getting elected, and he cannot perform his desired functions without maintaining that position, so he quickly learns to play the game by the rules and practices under which it has evolved.

The concept of Citizen Representatives was a carefully chosen construct, designed to protect against such corrupting influence. Men who come to government to serve their friends and neighbors for a brief period of time, but then return to their homes to conduct their own primary affairs view the world differently than men whose primary interests are furthering their political future.

Men who view governmental power as a goal to be fervently sought and vehemently defended and who arrive in office beholden to supporters lobbying aggressively for favors, which in this day and age encompasses all politicians, will find it hard to make difficult, often painful, decisions without first checking carefully to see which way the wind blows.

"To be successful, a politician has to appear hugely concerned with bettering the lives of ordinary citizens but be careful to avoid acting on those concerns so aggressively that they threaten the interests of the business elite."

— Michael Kelly (1957-2003)

"It used to be that influence peddling was hidden because people thought it was unacceptable. Now it's a formal part of the system."
— Fred Wertheimer (1939-)

"Came to do good and stayed to do well."
— Anonymous

One of the key roles of management is the responsibility for making difficult, sometimes painful decisions: evaluating conflicting facts, changing circumstances, alternative potential outcomes, potential unforeseen consequences, and balancing competing interests and rights – in short, applying wisdom and judgment with integrity. These are the roles of government. The role of government is the management of society.

When the role of business management is not clearly defined, understood and incented very often bad things happen. I have a cynical friend, also engaged in working with distressed and troubled companies, who posits that the prime objective of executive management is to "maintain their personal power and income". His view may be skewed by constant contact with troubled businesses, but looking at the composition of boards of directors and resulting compensation practices of many large public companies it is hard to argue very convincingly against him.

So it is with government. To the extent we choose, measure and reward our politicians based upon their success in fundraising and encourage them to build personal careers feeding endlessly at the public trough – that is what they will focus on. That is what they will learn to do best. The underlying work of government, the task of seeking and administering to a "more perfect Union", will remain secondary to the achievements which we reward.

Citizen Representatives could more readily be expected to serve on behalf of the common good. Professional politicians can only be expected to serve the fractured constituencies they cobble together to build and protect their electoral majorities.

Wish #2. Banish Multimillion Dollar Political Campaigns

The bane of professional politicians has been grotesquely exacerbated by the rapidly accelerating cost of the process. The Center for Responsive Politics reported that the aggregate spending for the 2008 electoral campaigns, including spending by candidates, parties and interest groups for the congressional and presidential races, was a record shattering $5.3 billion, up 27% from 2004. It was $2.4 billion for the presidential race alone. Total voter turnout for those elections was 132.6 million. To some, perhaps, the cost per voter of $18.10 for the presidential race or approximately $40.00 overall may not seem too outrageous. But it is insane to think that candidates can be required to beg and borrow sums of this magnitude without both a) unduly influencing their judgment, and b) causing them to lose any reasonable understanding of the value of money.

> *"One question, among the many others raised in recent weeks, had to do with whether my financial support in any way influenced several political figures to take up my cause. I want to say in the most forceful way I can: I certainly hope so."*
> — Charles Keating (1923-)

> *"Money buys access; access buys influence."*
> — Elizabeth Drew (1935-)

Unless it is done blindly and indiscriminately, all individual or group political funding is advocacy funding. Everyone who contributes to one candidate rather than another is expressing a choice and position, which brings us to an interesting dilemma. How can we reduce purchased political influence without impinging upon our rights of free speech? To date, the public arguments in resistance to campaign finance reform have been characterized as protections for free speech and have, as such, effectively obstructed all efforts for meaningful reform.

That would be fine, if it weren't a specious argument. No one is seeking to abrogate legitimate free speech. No one is going to be jailed for expressing seditious opinions. Printing presses are not going to be smashed. Broadcast licenses are not going to be revoked. By seeking to limit personal or corporate[5] campaign finance contributions or implement other reforms, no one is advocating shutting down the interchange of ideas.

---

[5] As an aside – Who was it who decided that corporations are protected by the First Amendment anyway? Take a poll of the American public. I doubt you will find 3 citizens out of 20 who think that a corporation, say GE, should be allowed to use its shareholders' assets to advocate on behalf of a specific candidate or policy. And if you do they'll all be either lawyers or lobbyists. Yet, subsequent to my initial draft of this section, the Supreme Court overturned some of the limited existing campaign finance restrictions on just this argument – that a corporation should be entitled to the rights of on individual as set forth in the Bill of Rights.

The facts as they exist today are remarkably simple and obvious. Those who contribute more get to speak louder – so much so that eventually the right to free speech becomes a right to buy control of the conversation and drown out the voice of the opposition. Placing reasonable limits and controls on campaign financing contributions in order to reduce both the appearance and actuality of unfair influence is not an abrogation of free speech.

Nevertheless, reasonable efforts to reform campaign finance and reduce political reliance upon advocacy financing continue to be fought from coast to coast by politicians and lobbyists for the simple reason that, winning is everything, and, as the game is currently played, it is easier to win with money than with ideas.

In part, this is simply an echo of my complaint against the professionalization of politics, which makes holding office a career imperative and thereby reinforces the influence of key campaign contributors over our representatives.

But, at heart, my concern is an increasing misunderstanding of the design of the American Democracy. Elected government officials are not supposed to be advocates for the portion of the electorate that voted for them. They are proxies for the electorate as a whole, indeed the nation as a whole, intended to serve by applying their wisdom, judgment and integrity. To some, it may seem a subtle distinction, but I see nothing subtle in it – our representatives should not view their job in Washington as rewarding the constituents who sent them there.

When politicians are forced to buy their way into office, and it is specious and silly to argue that requiring them to engage in multi-million dollar adversarial campaigns can be construed as anything other than forcing them to buy their way into office, it is naïve and irrational to expect them to arrive there without being indebted to their contributors. That forced indebtedness is damaging to the governmental process.

America, today as always, is facing difficult decisions requiring wisdom, judgment and integrity. When possession of office is one's goal, and the obtainment of office has been achieved only at exorbitant cost by the grace and support of highly segmented constituencies – *each pressuring aggressively for favorable treatment*, it is difficult to imagine how anyone could keep his judgment from being clouded.

Congress was not intended to become an adversarial battlefield, whereon "to the victor go the spoils". We should not be sending our representatives to Washington to "bring back the bacon", but to protect our rights and even-handedly advance the collective interests of the Republic. If, as I suggest, government is the management of society, then we need them to be free from obligations to narrow special interests so they may freely exercise their wisdom and judgment.

Dissemination of information and ideas is easier, and potentially cheaper, today than it has ever been. Utilizing the internet and public broadcasting, it would be easy to set aside and publicly fund forums for fair access and information exchange. We could choose to break the cycle of widely escalating costs which provides the lever for undue influence on policy from preferred constituencies. But we choose not to do so, because the exchange of money and power is the glue that holds the political machine together.

The combination of political careerism with multi-million dollar campaign funding requirements provides irresistible incentives and opportunities to convert political service into pay-for-hire advocacy.

> *"What do you suppose they are in Congress for,*
> *if it ain't to split up the swag?"*
> — Will Rogers (1879-1935)

We've created a class of professional politicians and immersed them in a system that forces them to beg financial favors from campaign contributors in order to keep their positions of power and status. Are we really so naïve as to think that those contributors don't ask, expect, demand and *receive* favorable consideration in return?

"The more heavily a man is supposed to be taxed, the more power he has to escape being taxed."
— Diogenes (412-324 BC)

"The subjects of every state ought to contribute towards the support of the government, as nearly as possible, in proportion to their respective abilities; that is, in proportion to the revenue which they respectively enjoy under the protection of the state."
— Adam Smith (1723-1790)
The Wealth of Nations 1776

"The only effective design for diminishing the income inequality inherent in capitalism is the progressive income tax."
— John Kenneth Galbraith (1908-2006)
Culture of Contentment 1992.

CHAPTER 4

THE MYTH OF PROGRESSIVE TAXES

If Warren Buffett and the Heinz-Kerry's and all of their peers pay lower tax rates than the average American, why is it we all think America has a progressive tax code? Because *we're a Nation of Liars*.

Our Government tells us we have a progressive tax code, publishing schedules which show a tiered rate that starts at 10% and currently maxes out at 35%. In public debate, our politicians argue vigorously about the merits or dangers of moving that top rate from 35% to 40%, scaling the tiers differently, implementing a millionaire's surcharge, or from time to time various other targeted tax increases they think might garner votes while not stifling campaign contributions.

On the Right, they cite the economic boom that followed the Reagan Revolution and argue that the progressive tax structures we now use are already too steep and constricting growth. They decry waging class warfare on the rich and suggest that still lower taxes are critical to America's continuing greatness. The Republican Leadership accepts no responsibility for their role in creating systemic budget deficits, continues to insist that tax reductions are the only path to growth and blames the deficit problem on a lack of disbursement controls – for which they also disavow responsibility.

From the Left, we hear that the average American is less well off today than he was twenty years ago, the gap between rich and poor is growing larger, and that if we don't start socking it to the rich the American Dream will remain nothing but an unattainable dream for all but the privileged few.

But neither side seems ready to step forward and address the question of whether or not we really have a progressive tax system. Apparently both sides are too embarrassed by the truth behind Buffett's accusation to dare to confront the question and explain how Buffet is paying only 18% of his income in taxes while his staff is paying 33%.

Wish #3. Banish Progressive Tax Rates

Progressive tax rates are a fraud, perpetrated upon the American public to obscure the various ways in which the tax code is used by politicians to protect the wealth of the elite and influential[6].

It is my opinion that the intricate calculations and manipulations of the tax code (exclusions, exceptions, deductions, multiple rates schedules, differentiation between employment and income taxes, et al.) are designed to maximize aggregate tax revenue while deliberately obscuring the basis, comparability, and sheer Machiavellian ingenuity of tax policies – thereby providing politicians a tool with which to fractionalize the population and reward their supportive constituencies.

> It's often been argued that income tax withholding is the most insidious political tool ever invented – that if the common man received his gross payroll up front and had to write a check to the government each week, no one would pay their lawful tax burden in full. A corollary to this observation could be that among the rich, for whom the details of exactly how much they are paying in taxes are generally more clear and obvious, that clarity and visibility provides a great incentive for them to ensure that they don't.

Trying to make sense of the conflicting allegations and understand the facts which drive our existing tax system can be frustratingly difficult.   I may be too cynical in this matter, but it's hard not to feel that our tax code, in its structure, execution and presentation, isn't just accidentally incomprehensible but has been designed to be deliberately misleading. This being the case, I regretfully concede it's unlikely that I can bring too much clarity to the situation in a few short pages of discussion. Nevertheless, I'm going to try[7].

---

[6] A reminder: I have been, and substantially remain a laissez faire capitalist and, despite any apparent disdain, I have a very strong desire to join the ranks of the elite and influential. It is not my desire or intention to suggest anything too damaging to the lucky few – since, like most of us, I'd like to join them.

[7] Caveat: I am not a trained economist, a professional statistician, or a licensed tax preparer. I cannot claim familiarity, access and knowledge of the best, most current or most reliable statistical databases. I have simply sought out, utilized and relied upon readily available public information from multiple sources. I have made a conscious effort not to knowingly utilize erroneous facts or twist them in support of my developing thesis and have tried, where most appropriate, to provide some reference to the sources used. But if you question the "facts" I cite, I urge you to challenge and research them independently. If you discover me to be wrong I would welcome hearing about it.

Broadly generalizing, I think most Americans believe that we utilize a progressive tax system that assesses a higher burden to those most able to pay while providing relief to those less fortunate. Likewise, broadly speaking, I believe that there is also a general consensus that it is appropriate to do so. Nevertheless, there is a great deal of debate as to what level of progressive assessments and minimum thresholds is optimal, and that debate is commonly accompanied by highly conflicting factual allegations which do not help to facilitate a more specific consensus.

Certainly, we are all aware that the income tax schedules do have a tiered and progressive rate schedule. But how does that play out in practice? How do you reconcile this general belief and consensus with Mr. Buffett's unrefuted claims? What are the facts?

A quick internet search of the term "tax distribution" revealed a multitude of factual citations and doomsday analyses, including the following:

> A site identified as www.twentysomethingsense.com ("tss.com") pointedly asks –
>
> **Did you know?...**
> The bottom 40% of income earners in the US collectively pay *negative* 3.8% of our overall tax burden?
> The middle 20% of income earners in the US collectively pay only 4.4% of our overall tax burden?
> The top 40% of income earners in the US collectively pay 99.4% of our overall tax burden?
>
> The Tax Policy Center ("TPC"), identified as a joint venture of the Urban Institute and the Brookings Institute, utilized a somewhat more data intensive and solemn chart presentation[8] to warn that:
> 46.9 % of all U.S. taxpayers will have zero or negative Income Tax Liability in 2009

These presentations are clearly driven by fear that soon over 50% of the population will be clamoring for more and more public services, secure in the knowledge that they will have no participation in paying for them. That could indeed be a cause for alarm, if it were true. But it's not.

---

[8] The cited TPC schedule can be found as Appendix I on page 206.

"If you torture them aggressively enough, statistics will confess to anything you tell them to say."

— Anonymous

The "facts", cited by tss.com and TPC, may be technically accurate, if you recognize that they are narrowly focused on Federal Income Tax, not "overall tax burden". But they do not represent a "true" picture of the U.S. tax base or burden.

Why do I say that? Let's focus first on a simple overview of Federal Tax receipts. According to the IRS[9] in 2009 total Revenue Collections, net of refunds, were $1.9 trillion, of which only 44.2%, or $843 million, represented Individual Income Tax.

United States Internal Revenue Collections - Net of Refunds Fiscal Year 2009		
	$Billions	**% of Total**
Individual Income Tax	$ 843	44.2 %
Employment Taxes	855	44.8 %
Corporation Income Tax	130	6.8 %
Excise Taxes	45	2.4 %
Estate Taxes	20	1.1 %
Estate & Trust Income Tax	11	0.6 %
Gift Taxes	3	0.2 %
Total Net Revenues	$ 1,908	100.0 %

As shown in the accompanying table, in 2009 Individual Income Taxes were not even the largest component of federal tax revenues, falling slightly behind the category of employment taxes, 98% of which represents Social Security and Medicare ("SS/Med") contributions[10]. These non-discretionary SS/Med "contributions" are assessed from the first dollar of earned income at a nominal rate of 7.65% of taxable wages, declining to 1.45% after taxable wages exceed a

[9] IRS.gov/taxstats IRS Data Book Table 1
[10] In 2007 and 2008 Individual Income Taxes were the largest component of Federal Tax Revenues. A three year history of summarized Federal, State and Local Tax Revenue is available for review in Appendix II starting on page 207.

substantial threshold ($97,500 in 2007)[11]. At first glance, therefore, it looks as though the "nearly 50% of the public" that we fear are paying no taxes are actually paying 7.65%. But as most of us know if we stop and think about it, that's just the employee contribution, which the employer matches with another 7.65%. Certainly we all recognize that our employers don't make that matching payment out of pure charity, but quite rationally consider it and all other wage-associated benefits to be part of each employee's total compensation. The description of the contribution as being shared between employer and employee is simply a polite fiction utilized by the government to obscure the real magnitude of the assessment. If we examine the tax relative to the full basis upon which it is being mandated and assessed, the effective tax rate on each employee's first $106,800 of FY2009 wages is 14.2%[12] for just Social Security and Medicare.

"But wait!", some will say, "Social Security and Medicare are retirement and medical savings programs – not taxes! They aren't contributing to paying for government services".

I vehemently dispute that… and refer you back to Chapter 2 (page 39).

Once again, I urge you to evaluate the facts for yourself with an open mind. Repeating my earlier observation, "Current Social Security contributions are being used to fund general governmental disbursements, including unsustainable operating deficits." Does that sound like either a savings or investment program? Are the promises of future Social Security benefits and Medicare coverage self-funded insurance programs? Or are they social programs being funded from general revenues? I believe they are social programs. Since the current contributions are not being escrowed and invested in tangible assets, and are backed by nothing other than the government's unsecured promise and its ability to raise future taxes or print more paper and inflate the currency, they should rightly be characterized as general revenues.

> Have I lost you yet? I hope not.
>
> If you don't yet see things as I'm describing them, I understand. But please stick with me. Changing one's world view is difficult and to the extent many of us have segmented these issues in our minds, accepted the formal rationalizations and definitions and "sipped the Kool Aid" as it were, it takes some time to give consideration to a different perspective.

---

[11] The threshold is adjusted periodically. It was $97,500 in 2007. In 2009/10 was and will be $106,800.

[12] For simplicity I have ignored the Earned Income Tax Credit which would shield individuals whose income is less than $7,550 per year and for those interested in the math the formula for the effective tax rate is Employee Contribution of 7.65% + Employer Contribution of 7.65% = 15.3%/Employee Gross of 100% + Employer Contribution of 7.65; or 15.3/107.65 = 14.2%.

If you need to, take a break, have a cup of tea, a beer, a walk… but please come back and stick with me for a bit. I'm trying to keep this short so that, if you determine afterwards I was nothing but a crank, I won't have wasted too much of your time. But the questions of how we as Americans are going to control our deficits and fund our governmental requirements are accelerating in importance and I'm trying to broaden the perspective of discussion. If, after you've processed my observations, you do still think I'm an idiot or a crank, perhaps you can initiate and guide a continuing conversation to show me where I've gone wrong.

Back to the perception that nearly 50% of the population does not bear "any of our overall tax burden". As noted above, The Tax Policy Center ("TPC") has warned that 46.9% of U.S. taxpayers will have zero or negative income tax liability in 2009. The notes accompanying that published finding indicate that it reflects the impact of new refundable tax credits signed into law by President Obama during his first year in office and will raise the rate from a previous level of 38%.

I can neither affirm nor challenge the accuracy of TPC's methodology and conclusions. However, my analysis of summary data (page 59) published by the IRS for the 2007 fiscal year[13] indicates that only 32.7% of tax filers had zero or negative tax liabilities in 2007 and that the average Adjusted Gross Income ("AGI") for 97% of these filers was less than $14,000.

If TPC is correct that the incidence of zero liability filers will increase to 47% that may indeed be an issue deserving of comment. But frankly, I'm not nearly as interested in trying to squeeze more out of people making as little as $14,000 per year as I am intrigued by a line item deeply buried in the IRS data which shows that in FY2007 2,606 filers with average AGI of $2.1 million escaped without paying any income tax.

More to the point, the *average effective income tax rate for **all filers paying tax was only 13.8%,*** an amount slightly less than the core SS/Med burden. Thus, while the *average taxpayer* did pay roughly twice the overall rate as individuals who fell below the income tax threshold, I still consider it a serious stretch to say that 47% of filers made no contribution to the overall tax burden.

But what about the marginal tax rates across the broad spectrum of the remaining taxpaying public? Surely there must be a steady progressive increase among this population as their earnings rise? Not really. If you doubt that, take a few minutes to study and absorb the next chart. Using FY2009 Tax tables it summarizes the income thresholds, progressive statutory rates, resulting taxes

---

[13] The most recent period available on their website as of the first week in May 2010

Selected Income and Tax Items
By Size of Adjusted Gross Income ("AGI")
FY2007

Size of AGI	# of Returns Millions	Percent of Returns	Percent Returns by Sub-Category	Adjusted Gross Income	Percent of Total AGI	Income Tax (Net of Credit) $ Billions	Percent of Total Income	Tax as Percent of AGI	Average AGI
Returns with Zero or Negative Tax									
Zero or Negative AGI	1.9	1.3%	4.1%	$(105)					$(55,189)
Under 50,000	43.4	30.4%	92.9%	621					14,309
$50,000 under $100,000	1.3	0.9%	2.8%	82					62,387
$100,000 under $500,000	0.1	0.1%	0.2%	12					139,542
Over $500,000 (a)	0.0	0.0%	0.0%	6					2,119,231
Subtotal Zero or Negative Tax	46.7	32.7%	100.0%	615	7.1%				13,176
Taxable Returns									
Zero or Negative AGI	0.0	0.0%	0.0%	(6)	-0.1%	0	0.0%	-1.7%	(1,161,000)
Under 50,000	48.5	33.9%	50.4%	1,327	15.3%	87	7.8%	6.5%	27,368
$50,000 under $100,000	29.9	20.9%	31.0%	2,128	24.5%	191	17.1%	9.0%	71,233
$100,000 under $200,000	13.4	9.4%	13.9%	1,784	20.5%	229	20.5%	12.8%	133,292
$200,000 under $500,000	3.5	2.4%	3.6%	1,002	11.5%	196	17.6%	19.6%	287,720
$500,000 under $1,000,000	0.6	0.5%	0.7%	440	5.1%	103	9.2%	23.4%	678,451
Over $1,000,000	0.4	0.3%	0.4%	1,397	16.1%	310	27.8%	22.2%	3,572,136
Total Taxable Returns	96.3	67.3%	100.0%	8,072	92.9%	1,116	100.0%	13.8%	83,852
Total Returns Filed	143.0	100%		$8,688	100%	$1,116	100%	12.8%	$60,763

(a) It is curious but unexplained how 2,606 filers with average AGI of $2.1 Million bore no tax liability.
Source: IRS.gov/stats, FY2007 Table 1.1. Most recent period available as of May 2010.

Federal Income and Social Security/Medicare Tax Burdens for Individual with up to $1,000,000 Earned Income
FY2009

Income Threshold			FEDERAL INCOME TAX			Social Security & Medicare		Combined Marginal Tax Burden	Cumulative Rate to Threshold
			Taxable Income	Federal Tax Rate 2009	Federal Income Tax	SS/Med Tax Rate	SS/Med Taxes		
						(a)		(a)	
$-	to	$8,350	$8,350	10%	$835	15.3%	$1,278	25.3%	25.3%
8,351	to	33,950	25,600	15%	3,840	15.3%	3,917	30.3%	29.1%
33,951	to	82,250	48,300	25%	12,075	15.3%	7,390	40.3%	35.7%
82,251	to	106,800	24,550	25%	6,138	15.3%	3,756	40.3%	36.7%
106,801	to	171,550	64,750	28%	18,130	2.9%	1,878	30.9%	34.5%
171,551	to	372,950	201,400	33%	66,462	2.9%	5,841	35.9%	35.3%
Greater than		372,950	627,050	35%	219,468	2.9%	18,184	37.9%	36.9%
			$1,000,000		$326,947		$42,243	$369,190	
Blended Tax Rate					32.7%		4.2%	36.9%	

Actual Effective Fed Tax Rate for Filers with AGI in excess of $1,000,000   22.2%

Difference   -10.5%

Discount from Earned Income Tax Schedules   -32.1%

Primary Source of Discount - Favorable Treatment of Capital Gains and Other Investment Income

(a) Includes Employee and employer contribution. Marginal rate is calculated versus Employee Gross income (not adjusted) and contributions and effective Federal Income Tax and SS/Med burden for a theoretical Individual with up to $1,000,000 of Earned Income.

The marginal tax burden for such an individual peaks at 40.3% when he reaches an earned income threshold of only $33,951, stays there until his income reaches $106,800, then **drops 9.4 percentage points** to 30.9% before ratcheting softly upward once again at thresholds of $171,501 and $372,951.

I'll repeat that. *The highest marginal federal tax burden, 40.3%, is imposed upon individuals with earned income between $33,950 and $106,800.*

An individual with as little as $34,000 of earned income has a marginal tax burden of 40.3%, while one making $1,000,000 has a marginal burden of 37.9%. When income reaches $82,000 the effective overall tax rate is 35.7%; at $1,000,000 it is 36.9%, only 1.2% higher. These effective rates do not reflect the magnitude of progressive differential that public policy discussions from either the right or the left would have us believe are the core tenet of our federal tax system.

Moreover this still depicts only a small part of the overall tax burden, since these rates apply only to *earned income*. They do not reflect the impact of preferred treatment on investment income, including reduced tax rates on capital gains and tax-free investment options, as well as state income taxes, and various other non-income taxes, all of which skew regressively against the less affluent portion of our society.

A less data intensive graphic presentation of a similar analysis appeared in an article published by the Journal of Economics and Finance Education ("JEFE") in the Summer of 2007[14] and is reprinted here.

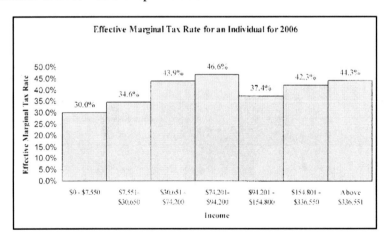

[14] "Introducing the Effective Marginal Tax Rate in Introductory Macroeconomics" by Stuart Allen, Geetha Vaidyanathan, Jeffrey Sarbaum; Journal of Economics and Finance Education, Volume 6, Number 1, Summer 2007.

It should be noted that changes in tax schedules between 2006 and 2009 resulted in some mild shifting of tax threshold levels, but the approximately 7 percentage point differential in the data between the preceding table and the graph from JEFE simply reflects provision for the impact of an assumed 7% state tax rate which was included in the JEFE analysis.

The results from the two analyses are essentially identical. Both demonstrate that the core of the middle class bears a higher marginal tax burden than the more privileged elite who ostensibly bear the brunt of a "progressive tax policy".

Moving on, let's follow JEFE's lead and broaden the perspective beyond Federal Revenues. What are the other tax obligations which burden the American public? According to data published by the U.S. Census Bureau, State and Local Tax Revenues in FY2009 totaled another $1.2 trillion as summarized in the following table.

National Totals of State and Local Tax Revenue
FY2009
$Billion

	State	Local	Combined
Individual Income Tax	$234	$17	$251
Corporation Net Income Tax	41	7	48
Property taxes	13	429	443
General Sales & Gross Receipts	221	61	283
Motor Fuels	36	1	37
Tobacco Products	17	0	17
Alcoholic Beverages	5	0	6
Motor Vehicle & Oper Licenses	22	2	23
All Other	97	30	127
Total	**$686**	**$547**	**$1,234**

As observed previously, the bulk of these state and local assessments cannot be viewed as anything but regressive. There may be some states which utilize a progressive income tax (though my home state of New Jersey does not) and buried under the category of All Other there is a small quantity of death and gift taxes, but the bulk of state and local taxes are consumption or transactional in nature and thus skew toward the less affluent who consume all of their earnings every year. Some people might argue that corporate taxes are a burden to only the more affluent community of shareholders, but I would remind them that, as with employer payroll contributions, the earnings themselves have been generated by the operating revenues of the corporation, thus the consuming public is really the party paying these taxes.

In summary then, where do we stand? The aggregate US tax burden in FY2009 was approximately $3.1 trillion, down from $3.6 trillion in 2008, representing roughly 22% of GDP and 39% of 2007 taxable Adjusted Gross Income ("AGI")[15]. The only significant portion of these taxes which can be argued to be progressively allocated is the portion of federal income tax generated by *"earned income"*. So how much is that? Someone can probably tell you, but it's buried so deep in the data that I couldn't reliably extract a precise figure.

Aggregate National Tax Burden Federal, State and Local
FY2009
$Billion

	Federal	State & Loocal	Combined	Percent of Total
Individual Income Tax	$843	$251	$1,094	34.8%
Employment taxes	855	-	855	27.2%
Corporation Net Income Tax	130	8	178	5.7%
Property taxes		443	443	14.1%
General Sales & Gross Receipts		283	283	9.0%
Motor Fuels		37	37	1.2%
Tobacco Products		17	17	0.5%
Alcoholic Beverages		6		0.2%
Motor Vehicle & Oper Licenses		23	23	0.7%
All Other	80	127	207	6.6%
Total	$1,908	$1,234	$3,142	100%
Percent of Total	61%	39%	100%	
Estim GDP			$14,200	
Tax as % of GDP	13.4%	8.7%	22.1%	
Aggreg. Adjusted Gross Income (2007)			$8,000	
Tax as % of 2007 AGI	23.9%	15.4%	39.3%	

Certainly aggregate earned income is substantially less than the roughly $8 trillion of Adjusted Gross Income which supplies the base for the federal income tax assessment. How do I know that? Because as personal AGI scales upward, actual effective tax rates do not track anywhere near the earned income rate schedules.

Extracting data from the Table on page 59, in FY2007 17.5 million returns were filed with AGI ranging between $100,000 and $1,000,000 in an aggregate

---

[15] Unfortunately, as of the first week in May 2010, the most recent published details of Income and Tax by AGI which was posted at IRS.gov/stats was for 2007, as shown in the schedule on page 57.

total of $3.2 trillion AGI. Those returns were assessed a total tax liability of $528 billion, an average rate of 16.4% (note I am here talking about only federal income tax liabilities, exclusive of SS/Med). But at the minimum $100,000 threshold for this group of filers, if AGI was taxed based upon earned income schedules, none of the filers would have had a minimum effective rate of less than 21.3%. The differential between this minimum threshold rate and the actual rate represents a discount of at least $157 billion, or 23% for this group of filers.

Similarly, in the smaller group of some 400,000 filers with AGI in excess of $1 million, taxes based on earned income schedules would have started at 32.8 % and scaled upward to approach the maximum 35% rate. The average actual tax rate for this group however was only 22.2%, fully 10.6% lower, yielding a minimum aggregate value discount of another $148 billion.

Using these broad assumptions as a driver, my rough estimate is that in 2007 less than $800 billion, approximately 1/5th of that year's total $3.6 trillion overall national tax burden, was generated from a progressive tax schedule. Unless I've lost the thread somewhere, despite the public pronouncements and general perception that we fund our government with a progressive tax system, only 20% of our overall tax burden is subject to tiered and progressive tax rates.

The bulk of our taxes are consumption oriented, thus regressively skewing toward those who consume all their income. The most fortunate and affluent among us receive preferential treatment in the form of caps on earnings subject to SS/Med contributions and reduced rates and approved shelters for returns on invested capital which far exceed the value of the progressively tiered income tax rates.

Although I suspect there are lots of economists out there who already know all this – it was surprisingly new news to me, as I expect it will be to many readers. It's not that the issues are new or unique, but the order of magnitude and significance of the issues is very hard to get your hands around. I confess it took me several days of diligent research and analysis before I felt I had made sense out of these details... even though I had a good idea where to look.

We have been told that we have a progressive tax system. We think we *ought* to have one. The fact that we don't, really, has been rather effectively obscured. I think deliberately.

As so clearly demonstrated by Warren Buffett's CEO Challenge and John Kerry's 2004 financial disclosures, the tax advantages provided to the wealthy are stunning in their scope and impact. Yet the silence shielding the magnitude of these advantages is deafening.

Returning back to the Kerry-Heinz disclosures which initially drew my attention to this issue, in the interest of providing fair treatment I must point out that the picture doesn't look any better versus Mr. Buffett. His reported $46 million income relates to an estimated $50 billion net worth, representing a return on assets of 0.09%, even less than the 0.5% return on assets I estimated for Mrs. Kerry. His roughly $8.3 million tax bill was thus only .016% of assets, thus the 8.3% of assets which I paid in federal taxes was a multiple of over *500 times* the tax rate paid by Mr. Buffet.

Is this really true? Is this possible? How is this possible? Certainly Mr. Buffett, who is a revered figure in the investment community, earned a higher return on his investments than 0.09% of assets. Didn't he?

Yes he did. But there's a difference between earnings and taxable income, a difference which constitutes the single biggest advantage that both the Heinz-Kerry's and Warren Buffett have over the bulk of the American public. Not only do capital gains receive favorable treatment in the form of reduced tax rates – *gains on assets are only realized and taxed upon sale.* So as long as you don't sell your assets their gains don't constitute income. As Mr. Buffett himself has stated on various occasions, the key to building wealth is the long-term compounding of tax free returns – a wealth accumulation advantage that Congress provides only to those lucky (already wealthy) investors who have no need to sell assets.

> In case you're wondering, I did not walk away from these realizations convinced that I needed to find myself a tax attorney and identify some way to hide or defer more income and shelter more of my assets from taxes. I still consider myself one of the lucky few. If I continue to work hard and do well there is a chance that before my death I might accumulate enough net worth to be subject to the estate tax[16] by the time I die. It's not very close yet, and it took a big step backward in September 2008, but I count it as one of my lifetime achievement goals, and the fact that I'm in the race to get there puts me in fairly exclusive company. Less than 2% of the U.S, population is expected to get there. A lot fewer, if you strike out those that got their wealth via inheritance.
>
> The core of the American Dream is the *opportunity* to start at the bottom (or middle) and rise to join this elite 2%.

---

[16] On 12/31/09 the existing estate tax exemption of $3.5 million was repealed, but it remains the subject of much debate, negotiation and potential for continuing change and manipulation. Unless I'm successful with this proposal, which suggests a replacement revenue source, I'm sure it will be back.

Back to my point. "Simpler and fairer" was the objective as defined by the WSJ. I agree with Mr. Buffett. He and his fellow Forbes 400 CEO peers don't pay their fair share in taxes. I agree with the Wall Street Journal. Tax policies need to be reformed to be both "simpler and fairer". But how is it supposed to get simpler and fairer if Senator Humphrey was stating the truth about the practices in the Federal Government where he served for 29 years? Or, even more importantly, if the only potential tax revenue sources considered by Congress continue to be either income taxes or still more regressive consumption taxes like sales taxes, an energy tax or a VAT (value added tax)? The WSJ may have focused on income tax rates and income shelters, but as I have periodically looked back on these disclosures, I have found myself scratching my head and beginning to think a bit more broadly and critically, wondering if maybe, as currently constructed, the tax system is even more inequitable than I had ever before considered?

Since 1913, when the Sixteenth Amendment was passed, removing limitations upon Congress' ability to levy a Federal Income Tax (initiated at a nominal 3%), the income tax has been viewed as the primary, if not sole, source of revenue for funding the services of government.

The public debate regarding income tax rates has raged on for years, focused almost entirely upon marginal rates, the highest tiered rates which are applicable to and assessed upon each incremental dollar of income. The argument says that when marginal rates get too high, they discourage work.

Even more vehement are the arguments, posited by many, many conservatives, citing reputable economists, that high tax rates on investment income discourage investment and result in slow growth. There are multiple broadly circulated findings suggesting that tax rate reductions change behaviors, stimulate growth, and generate higher tax revenues despite the lower rates. These are the arguments that have served as justification for negating the impact of progressive income tax rates by providing preferential treatment for investment income.

But perhaps it's the structure and implementation of those business and investment taxes that is causing the problem? Perhaps it is a result of modifying the form and basis of these taxes, making them taxes on income and profits rather than assets, that discourages investment?

Prior to 1913, the primary sources of government revenues had been assessments based upon assets, accumulated wealth and capital, which represented both the valued drivers of future earnings and a measurable indication of a citizen's ability to pay. But subsequent to the first implementation of the income tax not only have assessments on wealth dropped sharply out of use, replaced by higher and higher taxes on earned income, but taxes on the earnings from investments have received increasingly more preferential treatment.

"We have a system that increasingly taxes work
and subsidizes non-work."
— Milton Friedman (1912-2006)

The unspoken questions that hang in the air from Mr. Friedman's observation need to be asked.

Why are we doing that?

Should we be doing that?

Are there simpler, fairer, more equitable ways to structure our tax code than we are presently utilizing?

According to Galbreath, the Keynesian economist, "The only effective design for diminishing the income inequality inherent in capitalism is the progressive income tax." The implication of that 1992 statement was that we have a progressive tax policy.

Based upon my analysis, that's simply not true.

Ponder this:

Annual fees and expenses charged by professional investment managers have a very broad range, perhaps ranging from as low as a flat 0.5% of assets to as much as 3.5% plus a sometimes hefty percentage of investment profits, depending upon the nature of the services and Investments being managed. Investment advice offered by The Motley Fool advises that management fees for actively managed mutual funds currently average about 1.6% per year, and have been climbing in recent years.

Thus, while it would be difficult to make a precise comparison, it appears quite safe to suggest that most of the very wealthy and privileged among us, including but not exclusive to the rarified strata of the Heinz-Kerry's and Mr. Buffet, pay more to the people who manage their assets (often with the express goal of avoiding taxes) than they pay in support of the government and society which supports and protects the value of those assets.

CHAPTER RECAP:

MYTH OF PROGRESSIVE TAXES

As I warned earlier, bringing clarity to our Byzantine tax code in a few short pages is a daunting task, and I apologize for the fact that some of the preceding chapter has been, even for me as author, rather tough going. But I believe it constitutes important perspective relative to the discussions to follow.

So here's a cheat sheet of key observations and conclusions stripped free of the muddy factual support citations and underlying discussion.

1) As Americans, we have been told that we have a Progressive Tax Code and we believe it is appropriate that we *should have* a Progressive Tax Code.
   - But *we don't*.
2) Only approximately 1/5th of our national tax burden is calculated based upon progressive rate schedules.
   - In 2007 aggregate annual Federal, State and Local Taxes totaled $3.7 trillion.
   - But only roughly $800 billion of annual federal income taxes were generated from earned income subject to progressive rate schedules.
3) The true nature of Social Security and Medicare/Medicaid contributions and liabilities are broadly misunderstood.
   - The core SS/Medicare contribution rate is actually 14.2%, exceeding the average federal income tax rate paid in 2007 of 13.8%.
   - Since current SS/Med contributions are not being escrowed and invested in tangible assets, and are backed by nothing other than the government's unsecured promise and its ability to raise future taxes

or print more paper and inflate the currency, they should rightly be characterized as general revenues.

♦ The caps on earnings subject to SS/Med contributions give back to the upper income brackets a benefit roughly equivalent to the incremental taxes extracted by the progressive tax rate schedule.

4) Whether by active intention to deceive, or their own confusion and lack of awareness, our political class perpetuates the fiction of Progressive Taxes, causing most conversations about potential reform to start from an erroneous base.

5) Preferential treatment of investment income and the exclusive focus upon taxing income, rather than wealth, provides enormous benefits to the affluent and elite and is a substantial obstacle to the *American Dream* of *Equal Opportunity*.

6) The working poor, who labor for a living, pay a tax rate twice as high, or higher, than the "idle rich", who support themselves with income from investments[17] rather than through their labor.

7) The very wealthy often pay less toward the support of the government and society which supports and protects the value of their assets than they do to the investment managers who tend them.

---

[17] Assuming the investment income is managed into the form of long-term capital gains.

"Give me a One-Armed Economist!"
— Harry Truman (1884-1972)

"Deficit spending is simply a scheme for the confiscation of wealth."
— Alan Greenspan (1926-   )

"Don't fret about this year's deficit; we actually need to run up federal debt right now and need to keep doing it until the economy is on a solid path to recovery."
— Paul Krugman (1953-   )

"Reagan proved deficits don't matter."
— Vice President Richard Cheney (1941-)

CHAPTER 5

DEFICIT SPENDING:
PROBLEM? OR ANSWER?

Is deficit spending paving the road to America's impending obscurity? Or is it a valuable tool of government required to stimulate the economy, magnify growth rates, and expand opportunities?

Harry Truman had a knack for turning a good phrase, but on this topic he was seeking to shoot the wrong messenger. While his two-armed economist advisors may have confused and complicated his decision-making process by providing cautions about alternative potential outcomes, the one-armed economists that surround us today, making contradictory pronouncements with un-nuanced certainty, are probably more dangerous. The reason is simple: quoting Paul Simon, the songwriter, not the Congressman, "A man hears what he wants to hear and disregards the rest".

Given a choice of expert opinions, who wouldn't pick the one that's least painful? Or politically more expedient? Unfortunately, Economics, a field that is perhaps more akin to philosophy than science, provides a wealth of options from which to choose. Want a painless option? Take a look around, you'll find an expert to recommend it for you.

Over the past century a variety of pressures and practices have led to politically expedient tinkering with national debt and tax policy until we have arrived at a point where our Congress engages in fiscal policies that the average ten year old could tell them are unsustainable.

SOME BACKGROUND

In his 1960 book *The Law and the Profits*, C. Northcote Parkinson described how major increases in government spending have historically been linked with wars. During wartime, governments tend to spend "whatever is required", first increasing national debts, and following that with tax increases to retire those debts. The dual purposes of Northcote's book (which, though dated in some respects, I recommend highly as an informative source of history and perspective) was an attempt to:

a) show that there were practical limits to how much revenue could be collected, and

b) argue in favor of reducing tax rates in effect in 1960 as a means of improving government and society.

For context, it's worth pointing out that during WW II the highest marginal tax rates exceeded 90% and at the time of Northcote's book marginal rates in the 70% range were common.

Central to his discussions was an axiom he coined and described as Parkinson's Second Law, "Expenditure rises to meet income!" He believed that government budgets responded the same way personal budgets do, namely that new pressing needs inevitably arise to absorb all available revenues. Northcote was essentially putting forth a call for government to break the pattern of absorbing all available revenues and normalize tax rates, at least to pre-war levels. He was, thus, (at least in my recollection) one of the lead voices of the economic theory and political movement that followed and set forth to, in essence, "reduce taxes as a means of controlling spending".

> *"Government does not tax to get the money it needs; government always finds a need for the money it gets."*
> — Ronald Reagan (1911-2004)

I don't believe Parkinson (or Reagan for that matter) ever contemplated the scope of profligacy that would follow. Wars are no longer the primary source of deficit spending requirements. Our deficits, current and future, are now being generated by unrestrained wishes and promises. The restraint that lower taxes were meant to impose never materialized, as Congress continues to use the power of the Treasury to fund the promises that keep them in office.

Although there are at least a few staunch Republicans who continue to chant the mantra that cutting taxes to starve the beast will constrain spending, it seems somehow quaintly naïve to still pretend that Congress, as presently constructed, is capable of restraining itself to spend only the money it gets. Widely decried though it may be, deficit spending has become the new norm.

Whether Congress has been seduced by voices arguing that existing deficits are readily manageable, or whether they are consciously using deficit spending and induced inflation as a wealth transfer mechanism, I cannot say. But the political machine has been corrupted to the point where it is effectively impossible to apply controls to spending.

There is of course a proper use, both public and private, for debt. However, funding long-term structural imbalances between current revenues and disbursements should not qualify.

Although economists seem committed to mystifying their field, it actually is quite useful and instructive to think of governmental budget options and choices in terms similar to those that apply to individuals. Some uses of debt are sound and clearly beneficial. Other uses are irresponsible and short-sighted, trading ephemeral current rewards for long-term burdens.

As an example: think in terms of what is typically an individual citizen's most expensive lifetime purchase – a home. Absent the availability of mortgage financing, the average citizen might never be able to afford a home purchase. But utilized with proper discretion, a home mortgage can allow the owner to amortize the cost of his home over an extended period of time during which the owner enjoys the benefits of occupancy while simultaneously accumulating equity, effectively saving for the future. This is the classic beneficial use of debt; it allows one to obtain value today for something which will be paid for over time – and in the best circumstance it increases the future value over time. Cars and large appliances, college tuitions, and other large expenditures which provide benefits over extended time periods are similarly candidates suitable for term financing – presuming that attention is paid to how much of current and future cash flow is being allocated to those commitments and how secure and reliable future cash flows are anticipated to be.

Conversely, individuals who utilize credit cards to fund purchases that do not provide long-term tangible value, e.g. Caribbean vacations or restaurant bills, are well-advised to pay off the balances every month – because using high-interest financing for non-productive purchases is not typically a sustainable practice. Yes, it does pull the benefit of the purchase forward, but it does not increase the overall benefit obtained, merely delays the payment date and increases the effective price by adding interest while it places a burden on future cash flows. Psychologically, while most people find it easy enough to shoulder long-term mortgage payments while they enjoy the benefit of living in their home, it's much less satisfying to make continuing payments today for products whose benefits have long since evaporated.

Perhaps others of my age will also remember a recurring quote from a cartoon character named Wimpy: "I will gladly pay you on Tuesday for a hamburger today."

This is a classic example of a poor credit option – from both sides. By Tuesday the purchaser is once again hungry, and the now-consumed product is neither delivering him continuing value, nor available for recovery by the seller in case of non-payment.

In the for-profit business world, where capital investment funded today serves as the base for future profitable endeavors, debt is often used as an engine to accelerate growth. A farmer buys a tractor to till and sow more acres. A manufacturer builds a factory in which he forges steel, assembles cars, manufactures toys, or engages in other productive enterprises. Properly utilized, debt financing not only accelerates the availability of funds, fueling economic growth, it can "leverage" the returns, effectively magnifying the profits available for return to the equity investors.

In governmental terms, wars, which must be fought today in order to provide current and future protections, are conceptually similar to home purchases or factory investments. They represent unusually large (theoretically one-time, non-recurring) expenses which need to be funded up-front but will provide value over time. Government funded public works and infrastructure investments undertaken in order to provide long-term benefits to society can be viewed in a similar manner; they are tasks that can't be fully funded with current cash flows but provide long-term benefits and are suitable candidates for payment over time.

So far so good. Viewed in this manner it's easy enough to see that there clearly are appropriate and beneficial uses of public debt. This is the perspective from which Krugman advises that *this year's deficit* doesn't matter. Because he views recession fighting as an extraordinary expense that is both immediately necessary and will provide future benefits to justify the future repayment obligations.

However, what about *next year's deficit*?

Certainly one may argue with Krugman regarding the magnitude and effectiveness of specific policies which he advocates, but his observation and opinion clearly is grounded in an understanding that deficit spending is a tool to be applied with discretion. After all, he does at least narrow his intention to *this year*. Vice President Cheney's dismissive attitude toward deficits, however, doesn't exhibit the same understanding.

In fairness to Cheney, it should be noted that his oft-quoted observation that "Reagan proved deficits don't matter", is not an observation about economics, but about politics. In its more complete context Cheney is reputed to have to continued and asserted that *"We won the midterms. This is our due."*

This, of course, is precisely my point and has nothing to do with offering fairness to Cheney. The decisions our current political class make about deficits, and as nearly as I can tell all the decisions involved in government, are driven by politics, not economics, not logic, not an underlying drive to create a more perfect union. If I wanted to be "fair" to Cheney, the only way I could do so would be to suggest that the quote *may not be true*. Because, assuming it is accurate, it's one of the most self-damning quotes ever uttered by a politician.

Political office in the American government is supposed to be a role of public service – not a position from which to enjoy the spoils of victory.

Unfortunately, I have no reason to believe that Cheney was misquoted and it doesn't appear that he is alone in his view. The political class uses office to reward itself, its fragmented electoral majorities, and its financial contributors – as well as to punish its enemies. No wonder the American public feels so disenfranchised.

Once you understand and accept that fundamental fact of political motivation, it becomes easy to see that, for the political class, deficits truly don't matter. Nothing matters, unless it provides political benefit. As a political judgment, Cheney's correct, deficits don't matter. They're easy to hide, hard to understand, and tomorrow's problem. Even better – we're surrounded by one-armed economists arguing both sides of the issue, so there will be plenty of cover when it all blows up.

> Do the words "Nobody saw it coming" ring a bell? How many Treasury or Federal Reserve officials got fired in the 4th Quarter of 2008? How many members of the Congressional Finance Committee resigned in shame? Yes, a few sacrificial financial company executives ended up drifting softly toward the earth under their golden parachutes. But in the public sector, the folks at the helm simply gained more power and influence.

Back to the deficit – as a matter of fiscal (as opposed to political) policy, might the answer to the question be different? What's the real impact of our structural deficits and accumulating debt? Is it, as some now suggest, a lurking doomsday bubble, threatening to drag us all down? It's hard to know. I'm not aware of any reliable rules of thumb for evaluating the capital structure of a national government. The U.S. government can't simply be viewed like an operating business and valued on a multiple of earnings or cash flow, if for no other reason than the fact it has no operating earnings or positive cash flow. It is running structural deficits which seem to be on a course toward unimpeded growth. Deficit growth. Not economic growth. But despite the general aura of concern, there are a great many conflicting opinions and few people who are really conversant with the problem seem intent upon shedding much light on it.

So I've tried to assemble a few facts.

The nominal interest bearing national debt is now roughly $12.3 trillion, slightly over 90% of GDP and heading rapidly north. The only time during the last century when the national debt exceeded 100% of GDP was during WWII (the three year period from 1945 to 1947) when it hit a peak of 121% in 1946. According to the Congressional Budget Office ("CBO") base-line budget projections from August 2009, the national debt will slightly exceed 100% in 2011 and 2012.

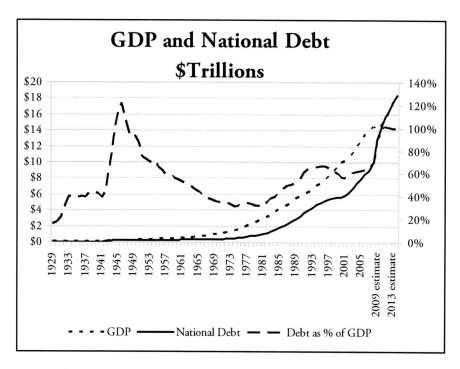

At today's historically depressed interest rates, the CBO budget indicates interest expense in 2009 and 2010 will be slightly under 5% of total disbursements – not too terrible a burden. However, those same CBO projections show debt rising 43% to $18.4 trillion in only five years with the interest burden nearly tripling to 12% of total disbursements in 2014, a somewhat less comforting picture.

Even more problematic, is the trend in off-balance sheet budget commitments. As I write this, a website titled USDEbtClock.org ticks furiously away delivering a cautionary message that our federal government's ever-rising *Unfunded Liabilities* now total $106,982,222,830,378. That's $106.9 trillion, with a "T". Presumably the lack of rounding in their calculation is designed to imply a measure of accuracy that I frankly doubt is real, but, nevertheless, their point does come across; the numbers are too big and rising too rapidly for most of us to even grasp.

Adding the more widely reported and acknowledged National Debt figure of $12.3 trillion, this yields a total obligation of $119.2 trillion, equal to 8.4 times FY2009 GDP and 57.0 times FY2009 estimated Gross Federal Revenues.

I'll restate that. If Gross Federal Revenues suddenly stopped growing, and 100% of their continuing collections were devoted to retiring the accrued value of known future liabilities, paying no future interest and leaving nothing available for continuing government services other than Social Security, prescription drugs and Medicare, *it would take 57 years to pay off those liabilities*.

That can't be good. Can it?

U. S. Debt Clock.org
Reported Unfunded Liability Balances
5:19 PM EST, January 15, 2010

Un-Funded Liabilities	$Trillion
Social Security	$ 14.1
Prescription Drug Liability	18.6
Medicare Liability	74.2
Total Unfunded Liabilities	106.9
U.S. National Debt	12.3
Combined Federal Liabilities	$ 119.2
Estimated FY2009 (a)	
- GDP	$ 14.1
- Gross Federal Revenue	$ 2.1
Comb Fed Liabilities as a multiple of:	
- GDP	8.4 X
- Gross Federal Revenue	56.8 X

(a) Source: OMB Budget Aug-09

But let's back up to just the interest bearing National Debt.... Based on current projections, how long would it take us to retire that?

As noted above, the current interest bearing debt is approximately $12.3 trillion, and it is projected to rise to $18.4 trillion at the end of 2014. Let's take that at face value and assume the OMB is correct and has not underestimated any of the new programs being put in place. I consider that a major leap of faith, but we have to start somewhere. Obviously, as currently forecast, there is no free cash flow available to retire debt, it's increasing. So now assume we want to get more aggressive and either cut spending or raise taxes, what would it take?

Let's examine cutting expenditures first.

For illustrative purposes and easy reference, I have reprinted hereafter a slightly modified version of a CBO Baseline Budget Table published in August 2009[18].

The OMB reports three primary lines of disbursements:

1) *Discretionary Spending* – spending subject to regular "appropriations" bills allocating specific approved disbursement sums, and
2) *Mandatory Spending* – spending controlled by laws that don't appropriate specific sums, but establish less flexible commitments for long-term entitlements.
3) Net Interest payments.

Over the first five year period, the mandatory disbursements total $10.3 trillion, of which $6.1 trillion is defined elsewhere as specifically related to three named programs: Social Security, Medicare and Medicaid – the so-called "third rail" issues of American politics. Let's assume then that the entire $10.3 trillion is off-limits and can't be cut.

What about the "Discretionary" programs? What's in there? $6.9 trillion over five years of which $3.7 trillion, over 53%, is Defense and $3.2 trillion is "Other". During that 5 year period total debt is forecast to go up by $4.8 trillion. So if we cut out 100% of our Defense and Other "Discretionary" programs, we would only reduce the debt by $2.1 trillion over five years. At that rate ***we could be debt free in only 30 years – assuming we closed down the government***.

Here again, please make your own judgments based upon the data, but in my view, so long as entitlement reform is off the table, no amount of cost cutting is going to make a significant dent in the national debt. Cut 25% of all discretionary spending for the next ten years and the total debt still goes up by $5.3 trillion and ends the period at 82% of GDP.

---

[18] For clarity I have suppressed the individual years 2010 – 2019, maintaining just the 5 Year and 10 Year summary columns, and to reduce potential confusion, I have added a line showing the OMB's projected Gross National Debt. In the original published schedule the OMB omitted the total National Debt, choosing to focus on only the Debt held by the Public and eliminating debt held in Government accounts – primarily the cumulative Social Security surpluses which the government has used to fund current operations. Does this imply a tacit agreement from the OMB that the SS/Med "Trust Fund" accounting is a meaningless optical trick? I'll let you use your own judgment on that.

Table 1-2.
CBO's Baseline Budget Projections
Aug-09

	Actual 2008	Estim 2009	5Years 2010- 2014	10Years 2010- 2019
	In Billions of Dollars			
Revenues				
Individual income taxes	1,146	918	7,122	17,425
Corporate income taxes	304	142	1,437	3,279
Social insurance taxes	900	889	5,055	11,245
Other revenues	174	152	1,000	2,229
Total Revenues	**2,524**	**2,100**	**14,614**	**34,177**
On-budget	1,866	1,447	10,998	26,084
Off-budget	658	653	3,616	8,093
Outlays				
Mandatory spending	1,595	2,270	10,222	22,630
Discretionary spending	1,135	1,241	6,797	13,929
Net interest	253	177	1,583	4,754
Int % of Total	8%	5%	9%	12%
Total Outlays	**2,983**	**3,688**	**18,602**	**41,314**
On-budget	2,508	3,168	15,627	34,530
Off-budget	475	520	2,974	6,784
Deficit (-) or Surplus	(459)	(1,587)	(3,988)	(7,137)
On-budget	(642)	(1,720)	(4,630)	(8,446)
% of OnBud Rev	-34%	-119%	-42%	-32%
Off-budget	183	133	642	1,310
Debt Held by the Public	5,803	7,612	11,439	14,324
Total National Debt (a)	**9,986**	**11,901**	**16,683**	**20,667**
Memorandum:				
Gross Domestic Product	14,222	14,140	79,103	176,828

(a) Gross National Debt was excluded from OMB Baseline summary in favor of Debt held by Public. Gross national debt incorporated by author from associated OMB schedule.

So now let's look at increasing taxes.

What's a reasonable goal? I admit, I haven't really come to grips yet with the conflicting views of how much deficit spending is desirable, but at this point I'm just trying to find some perspective on the issue. So, for the purposes of perspective, I'm going to arbitrarily set an objective target of reducing the national debt to no more than 50% of GDP. The CBO forecasts GDP in 2019 to be $21.1 trillion.

I don't have a better number, so I'll use theirs. In order to reach our target 50% of GDP, we need to reduce the projected debt by $10.1 trillion. Ignoring interest and inflation, in order to accomplish that over the ten year forecast period it would require an additional $1.0 trillion increase in annual revenue. Targeting a 30 year reduction would require $330 billion per year. Again, these are highly imprecise figures, set forth for perspective, not argument.

What do they tell us?

Estimated 2009 gross federal revenues as shown in the August baseline projections totaled $2.1 trillion as shown in the following table. Thus, normalizing debt levels over a 10 year period would require almost a 50% increase in total federal revenues. That sounds pretty painful.

Estimated Federal Revenue 2009	
	$Billions
Individual Income Taxes	$ 918
Corporate income Taxes	142
Social Insurance Taxes	889
Other Revenues	152
Total Federal Revenues	$ 2,100
Source: CBO Baseline Budget projections; Aug-09	

So let's treat it like a home mortgage. Paying it down in equal increments over 30 years would require a 15% revenue increase – not a happy prospect, but a bit more reasonable.

Unfortunately, it's not that simple, because the $2.1 trillion gross revenue includes $889 billion in SS/Med contributions. If we attempt to maintain the fiction that SS/Med are not part of general revenues, the required percentage increase in income and other taxes jumps back up to a 27% increase – and *every time Congress chooses to exempt another of its favored constituencies the burden on the remaining taxpayers gets bigger*. If you raise the $330 billion entirely from personal income taxes it jumps back up to a whopping 36% increase.

I could go on trying to analyze the budget in greater detail, but it hardly seems necessary; it would just imply a greater level of specificity and understanding than is realistically justifiable. Except as directional indicators and planning tools, ten year forecasts often aren't worth the paper on which they're printed. The preceding analysis is intended simply to provide perspective upon the near term – by which I mean the ten-year future, and in summary my observations are fairly simple:

- Deficit spending and the national debt have been rising with only nominal interruption since 1981.
- The national debt is rapidly approaching 100% of GDP, a level not experienced since WWII.
- Current ten year forecasts show debt levels stabilizing at roughly 100% of GDP, but no reductions.

A return to more normalized debt levels cannot be achieved without pain: service and cost reductions and/or revenue increases of *a magnitude which our current political class refuses to even discuss.*

More subjectively, I might add my opinion that the "stabilization" of debt as shown in the OMB ten year forecast seems more grounded in wishful thinking than any identified policy or evidence of change in the existing trend.

The long-term future is even more dismal. But here there is no need to bore anyone with independent analysis since there is so little disagreement on the matter and I can simply quote from an OMB summary of Economic Assumptions and Analyses published on the White House website[19]. Buried deep within, on page 191, I quote their observations with regard to the impact of long-term Medicare, Medicaid and Social Security programs which they include under a section heading entitled *"An Unsustainable Path"*.

"The overall budget cannot sustain the projected increase in these major programs without policy changes."

Extracting from the OMB's Table 13-2 which they publish in support of that observation, the OMB projects Federal Debt held by the Public[20] rising from 35% of GDP in 2000 to 67% in 2010 and 119% in 2040.

Have you noticed many politicians making a legitimate attempt to step forward and lead a principled discussion of these issues? Neither have I. Instead, we're "rearranging the deck chairs": pretending our recent health care legislation is addressing the "cost curve" when it's really just increasing entitlements and

---

[19] http://www.whitehouse.gov/omb/budget/Analytical_Perspectives/
[20] Note once again the OMB Table displays only Debt Held by the Public, not the more familiar total national debt which is already approaching 100% today.

"taking advantage of the crisis" to promise universal access to structurally unsound programs.

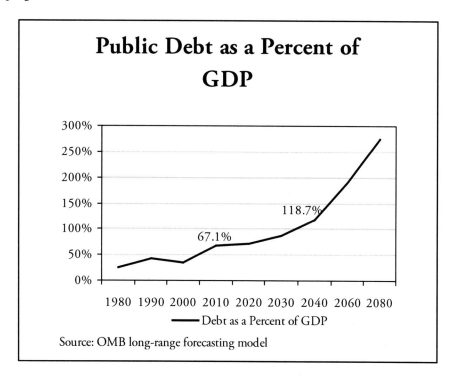

Public Debt as a Percent of GDP

67.1%

118.7%

Debt as a Percent of GDP

Source: OMB long-range forecasting model

Don't you just love to watch government in action?

Although this is the first time I have ever attempted to read and absorb the OMB budget, I have no reason to believe this is the first time these cautionary observations about "An Unsustainable Path" have been published. We hear about it so regularly that we are largely inured to it.

In 2008 Pete Peterson, Senior Chairman of The Blackstone Group and former U.S. Commerce Secretary, committed $1 billion and formed the Peter G. Peterson Foundation, dedicated to "increasing public awareness of the nature and urgency of key fiscal challenges threatening America's future", issues which *he has been personally championing for over thirty years.* His first book on the topic, *"On Borrowed Time"*, was published in 1988. But the message doesn't seem to be getting through.

While our political class certainly can't claim a lack of awareness, they exhibit no political will to meaningfully address the problem. This isn't called a "third-rail" issue by accident.

THE ROLE OF INFLATION

At the outset of this chapter I included a quote from Alan Greenspan, describing deficit spending as a "scheme for the confiscation of wealth"[21] – a particularly harsh assessment of the role that deficit spending plays relative to inflation, offered in 1966 by a man who would later serve as Chairman of the Federal Reserve charged with fighting inflation for 19 years (1987 – 2006). But what exactly was Greenspan's point? In a nutshell, he charged that "governments confiscate the wealth of the productive members of a society to support a wide variety of welfare schemes", but that since it was politically unpalatable to do so entirely by taxation, by unlinking from the gold standard and simply printing more money the government could utilize deficits to fund their programs[22]. However, the result would be inflation, dilution in the value of the currency, i.e. the "confiscation of wealth".

As illustration, I've utilized data provided by the Bureau of Economic Data and the OMB to graph the change in value of the currency in constant Dollars (2009 equals 1:1) from 1929 to 2009.

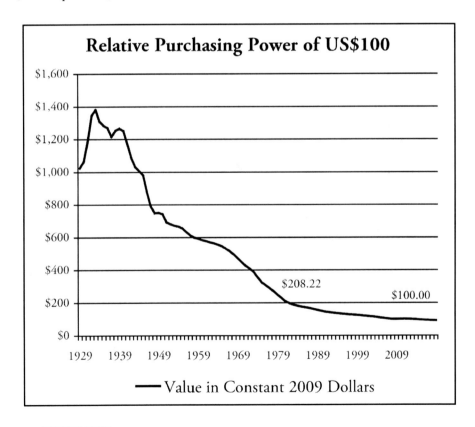

---

[21] Gold and Economic Freedom, by Alan Greenspan, published in 1966.
[22] Don't misinterpret my description, he was not advocating this policy, but warning against it.

In the eighty year period between 1929 and 2009, the US Dollar lost 90% of its purchasing value. Measuring from 1981 to 2009, the most recent 28 year period of relatively consistent debt growth, it lost 52% of its purchasing value. For those of you who like to keep score, during Alan Greenspan's 19 year tenure at the Fed from 1987 to 2006, it lost 40% of its purchasing value.

Buried amongst the charts included with the OMB budget is a chained price index from which it is possible to calculate that the OMB assumes the dollar will lose another 16% of its purchasing value over the next 10 years.

I have to be honest here. My head hurts every time I try to get my mind around this stuff. But I keep trying to bring this into focus and perspective. What does it really mean? Here are a couple of key questions that arose in my mind regarding this budget assumption.

Item 1: Are these inflation assumptions likely to be accurate?

Not under current policies.

Assume the OMB is correct and inflation is held to only 16% over the 10 year forecast. Then assume they repeat that performance for another ten years. That means the purchasing value of the currency will decline by only 30% over 20 years.

Good job… if they can do it. That would be roughly 25% better than the performance during Greenspan's 19 year seat at the helm – despite debt levels which are spiking substantially higher.

That would be an exceptionally good trick…. simultaneously running higher deficits and lower inflation. But it seems to run counter to the prevailing economic theories, so *I'm a serious skeptic.*

I can't imagine anybody at the OMB really believes that under current trends future inflation is going to be less than recent historic trends… and if they do I want to know what they've been smoking.

Item 2: What is the underlying cost/benefit derived from inflation?

The theoretical "upside" of inflating the currency is that it reduces the cost of the national debt. Applying a 16% decline in value to our existing $12 trillion debt yields a $1.9 trillion benefit; using Greenspan's logic cited above, we will thus have eliminated the need to impose $1.9 trillion of incremental taxes.

But at what cost?

Even assuming an unrealistically nominal 2% interest rate, carrying that existing $12 trillion in debt for 10 years will cost $2.4 trillion. So we pay $2.4 trillion in interest in order to save $1.9 trillion? I fail to see a compelling logic here.

Worse yet, a quick glance at the Q3 2009 Federal Reserve Statistical Release revealed non-governmental entities holding $44.4 trillion in financial assets[23]. Applying the same 16% across these dollar denominated financial instruments suggests a *$7.1 trillion decline in the underlying value of those holdings.* When someone observes to me that planned inflation is an effective tool for minimizing the damage of the national debt it is clear to me that one of us doesn't really understand the issue.

As I said, trying to work this through makes my head hurt, so, since I have little reason to believe that the average Congressman is that much smarter than I am, I'm sympathetic to the fact that the average Congressman probably tries to think about it as little as possible.

After all, if the forecasts may not be worth the paper they're written on, why worry about them?

Because:

1. By ignoring the need to balance the budget it probably costs the public $7.1 trillion to suppress taxes by $1.9 trillion.

2. There appears to be no dispute that we are on "An Unsustainable Path".

3. Those among us who have passed the age of 50 should be aware that a 30 to 40 year time horizon isn't really that long.

That being the case, I don't think it's unreasonable that we, as citizens, start demanding our politicians pay a bit more attention to driving the bus. We cannot allow our political class to continue to operate without thinking beyond a two, four or six year election cycle.

---

[23] Composed of $12.1 trillion deposits and credit instruments, $12.7 trillion pension and life insurance reserves, $13.9 trillion corporate equities and equity in non-corporate businesses, $4.2 trillion mutual funds, $1.5 trillion other.

PART III

WHAT'S
REALLY IMPORTANT?

"Democracy is two wolves and a lamb voting on what to have for lunch"
— Benjamin Franklin (1705-1790)

"A democracy is nothing more than mob rule, where fifty-one percent of the people may take away the rights of the other forty-nine."
— Thomas Jefferson (1743-1826)

"Democracy never lasts long. It soon wastes, exhausts, and murders itself. There never was a democracy yet that did not commit suicide."
— John Adams (1735-1826)

"Democracy is the worst form of government except for all those others that have been tried."
— Winston Churchill (1874-1965)

CHAPTER 6

REQUIREMENTS OF OUR AMERICAN DEMOCRACY

Have you noticed that every time I want to change topics I have to start by addressing a widely believed fallacy?

Here comes a big one.

Way back when I was in junior high school, what's known as middle school today, either I wasn't paying attention or somebody lied to me. It is of course possible I wasn't paying attention. I was a budding teenage boy and, like most of that ilk, unless you stuck to two fairly obvious topics my attention span was pretty short. But I don't think I'm the only one who came away from my early civics lessons with this particular misunderstanding.

I keep referring to this "American Democracy". That's a misnomer. America is not a Democracy. At least it wasn't intended to be. It's a Republic… and the difference is important.

> *"There is no good government but what is Republican… the very definition of a Republic is 'an empire of laws, and not of men'."*
> — John Adams (1735-1826)

Take careful note of the quotes that open this chapter. It's clear that the founders were intently focused on protecting America from the abuses that often come from the power politics of unfettered majority rule.

> *"We are a Republican Government. Real liberty is never found in despotism or in the extremes of Democracy... It has been observed that a pure democracy, if it were practicable, would be the most perfect government. Experience has proved that no position is more false than this. The ancient democracies in which the people themselves deliberated never possessed one good feature of government. Their very character was tyranny; their figure deformity."*
> — Alexander Hamilton (1755-1804)

I'm pretty sure I never heard that quoted when I was in the seventh grade.

For the record, I'm not going to stop referring to America as a Democracy, partly because old habits die hard and partly because the elements of Democracy upon which our Republic is built are very strong. But the caveats and cautions of our founders are important to remember and central to sound government.

The genius of the American government is its establishment and protection of individual rights and its dedication to providing equal opportunity to all of its citizens. Tyranny is the enemy, whether that be the tyranny of a king, a privileged elite, or a majority vote over who's for lunch. The first responsibility of the U.S. Government is to protect the rights of its citizens. Take a moment and let that sink in.

The proper role of our government is *not to impose the will of the majority*.

So, having dealt with that definitional issue, "What are the key requirements of "Our American Democracy"? I cite four.

1. REPRESENTATIVE GOVERNMENT

Forgive me if I seem to be recovering ground previously addressed, but the issues and distinctions here are more subtle than they seem and they deserve both elaboration and reinforcement. (I have an uncle who's a teacher and he advised me once that new ideas have to be reinforced at least seven times before they sink in. I'll try not to go that far.)

The issue of importance is coming to grips with the specific kind of representation our American Democracy requires, and not settling for anything less.

There are (at least) two ways to view what it means to elect representative government. At their core, I would describe the options as:

- choosing someone to act upon direct instructions, versus
- authorizing someone to utilize best judgment in acting upon our behalf.

Putting it another way, it's the difference between granting a "Limited" versus a "Broad" Power of Attorney: *executing the will of the majority* versus *exercising judgment on behalf of the people.*

When we send an electoral delegate to go to the national convention to represent our state, we are implicitly sending them to reiterate our state-wide vote. We would be appropriately shocked and infuriated if he/she got there and switched our Democratic vote to Republican. Most of us aren't even aware that there are situations in which that electoral delegate has discretion to do anything other than reiterate our specific vote. (There are.) Electoral delegates are clearly intended to simply execute the will of the majority.

But when we send our representative to serve in the House or Senate, the scope of responsibilities which he/she will be entrusted to act upon are far wider than any specific instructions we have provided. He/she will be exercising judgment. That being the case, the key questions are, "On what basis?" and "On whose behalf?"

> *"There is no qualification for government but virtue and wisdom."*
> — Edmund Burke (1729-1797)

It is my opinion (and I do recognize that it is opinion and thus subject to potential debate and disagreement) that our institutions cannot function properly when our representatives view their responsibility and/or choose to act in the interests of anything more narrow than the population as a whole.

In order for our government to function in an optimal manner, as intended, we need our representatives to be fully aligned with our society and acting on our collective behalf. They need to be *"Citizen Representatives"*, whose personal interests, as much as possible, are coincident with the population as a whole. They need to understand and respect that as their responsibility. As soon as they lose that understanding and start focusing upon narrow divergent interests, whether interests of fractional constituents or their own personal desires and benefits, the workings of government begin to be distorted.

It is difficult to fulfill this requirement when we fill our government with professionals. I won't restate all the observations made in Chapter 3, but the designed requirement of our government, the need for our representatives to exercise balanced judgment on behalf of the common good, is not well served by the process we have developed to choose them or the atmosphere in which we make them work. When our politicians view their vote as a tool with which to curry favor and support from their constituents, they undermine the process of good government.

Our elected representative government, as conceived in the U.S. Constitution, was not supposed to be composed of entrenched ruling elites. But reelection rates exceed 90% and the pool from which our candidates are chosen is surrounded by a towering barrier fence in the form of twin obstacles: money and influence. (Oops! That's redundant.)

Neither was our government intended to be a competitive playing field, populated by adversarial factions seeking to dominate the opposition. However, even the casual observer of its operations can scarcely fail to notice that winning and losing, seizing and holding power, seem to be of far greater importance to both our political class and the pundits who watch them than the quality of leadership and governance they provide.

> According to information posted on DailyPaul.com, 54 Senators and 162 Representatives, thus forty percent of a total 541 Members of Congress (including 6 non-voting Representatives) identify their profession as lawyer or attorney. The number may well be larger, since the body may include lawyers by training who do not view that as their profession.
>
> Refraining from the temptation to recite a bunch of cheap, "How many lawyer… " jokes, I find myself asking, "What are the implications of this fact?" Might there be any unintended detrimental consequences? Certainly, it demonstrates an over-weighted representation relative to the population as a whole which would seem to be consistent with the general concentration of privilege, education and money which we all must recognize pervades the Congressional bodies.
>
> But my concern is more specific. By training, lawyers are steeped in a doctrine which tends to make them agnostic toward truth. Their canon is that both sides in any adversarial conflict, whether guilty or innocent, deserve the best possible

representation; the lawyer's job is not justice, it is *seeking to win*, the jury determines guilt or innocence.

This may be a sound and viable way to ensure equal representation before the law, but I'm not as confident that it facilitates good government.

The work of government is a solemn, civic responsibility which requires the utmost honesty and integrity be applied to the exercise of judgment. All obstacles to that objective are obstacles to good government. One of the key obstacles is that our elected officials no longer look or act very much like the Citizen Representatives who were intended to populate the halls of Congress.

2. EQUAL OPPORTUNITY REQUIRES EQUAL TREATMENT

No matter how well intentioned, the creation of any favored constituency is anathema to the goal of equal opportunity, which I view to be the central tenet of our national ideal and the struggle toward a more perfect union. The establishment of favored classes or perpetuation of privileged elites tears at the foundations of our society. It sows the seeds of discontent, entitlement and dishonesty. After all, few people actually acknowledge to themselves when they are being dishonest. In order for most of us to engage in public dishonesty we must first start with self-delusion. When we enact public policies which reinforce those delusions, which is precisely what we accomplish when we institutionalize unequal treatment, we tilt the playing field and upset the balance, stability, and collective judgment of our society.

I may be overlooking something, but I can personally not think of a single other factor which is so effective in warping one's judgment than the concept that "different rules should apply to me".

Discontent. Entitlement. Dishonesty. One grows out of the other. "He's being treated better than I am." "I deserve more than I'm getting." "I'm not receiving unequal treatment. I deserve to be treated like this." Once that sense of entitlement begins to take hold it begins to morph, step by step, into an accelerating litany of self-congratulation and self-delusion. Arguably, that self-congratulatory delusion may have reached its pinnacle on November 8th, 2009 when a headline in the *Times of London* appeared to quote Lloyd Blankfein, CEO of Goldman Sachs saying, "I'm doing God's work"[24].

Challenged to justify Goldman Sachs' compensation practices, it is clear that Blankfein has not the slightest sense of doubt, discomfort, or concern that what

---

[24] Though "God's Work" was set in quotes above Mr. Goldfein's picture, in reading the article it appears his actual words offered in justifying the anticipated $700,000 average 2009 compensation for Goldman's 30,000 employees, were, "We have a social purpose".

they are doing is either wrong or in some way "inequitable". He views himself and his firm as an important contributor to a "virtuous cycle" of wealth creation that apparently "entitles" him and his associates to be treated as Masters of the Universe.

Think about it. From *discontent...* to *entitlement*. It is astounding how easy it is for a man who has managed to overcome the odds and obstacles to suddenly see the benefits of privilege in a totally different, far more favorable light. Worse yet, it is an ugly, slippery slope from these perception-warping emotions to *dishonesty*.

Please understand, I am not accusing Blankfein (or his associates at Goldman Sachs, contemporaries throughout Wall Street, or enablers in Congress and the Fed) of being "dishonest" in any legal sense. Delusional, absolutely; but one can be intellectually dishonest without breaking any laws.

What I am describing as "dishonesty" is not frequently exhibited by the breaking of laws, but by making laws: codifying preferential laws and regulations and rationalizing preferential policies. What I am referring to is *intellectual* dishonesty, characterized by self-justifying rationalizations, an ivory-tower seat of privilege, and a sometimes willfully distorted view of the facts.

As demonstrated in Chapter 4, despite the substantial effort expended by our political and financial elites to mischaracterize our tax system as "progressive", *working class Americans with income ranging from $33,950 to $106,800 are subject to higher marginal tax rates on their wages and salaries than Lloyd Blankfein with his reported $26 million 2009 compensation package* – even before one factors in favorable treatment he undoubtedly receives for capital gains, tax-sheltered benefits, deductions and exclusions, etc.

> Note that while I use Goldman Sachs as a high visibility example, it is not specific individual or corporate compensation practices of which I disapprove, but the incestuous and inequitable relationships that exist between the professional and political elites which have made this kind of entitlement thinking and policy possible.
>
> In addition to the tax rate issues already discussed, the variety and ingenuity of ways our government has favored the financial establishment over the past year, is astounding.
>
> As example: while Blankfein is patting himself on the back for his firm's superior 2009 performance, I find myself forced to suggest that much of the phenomenal bounce-back in financial firm profitability across the industry was not a result of value added performance, but was externally, largely governmentally, produced.

- When the Fed responded to the financial crisis by providing financial firms with unprecedented   free-money, near zero-interest policies, did those firms reduce consumer credit card rates? Or commercial loan interest? No. They booked massive profits.... often after raising interest and fees they charged to their customers.
- When the crisis forced some holders of securities to sell illiquid assets at distressed prices how hard was it for the buyers of those securities to make exorbitant profits? When a security with an intrinsic value of 50% of face value is subject to forced sale at 30%, how smart does a buyer have to be to make money on the trade? Particularly when the Government is providing zero percent funding to encourage the transaction?
- How much of 2009 financial firm profits came as a result of the Government stepping in to fund insolvent insurer AIG? It is generally acknowledged that evaluating potential non-performance of one's counterparty is a risk borne by the contract holder. Not so for financial firms in 2008/2009.

Back to Equal Treatment: Presumably few Americans would dispute that equal treatment is a requirement of sound government, at least when it is stated in relation to a functioning and reliable judicial system. I'm not sure I've ever heard anyone argue against the concept of every man's right to "Equal Treatment Under the Law". On those occasions where either facts or perceptions suggest that the law has not functioned in such a manner, whether in response to a presidential pardon, high profile murder acquittal, or statistical evidence of discriminatory sentencing disparities across racial profiles, there arises a chorus of righteous indignation. Alternative views of such matters of judicial conduct and function may be loudly debated based upon perceptions of the facts, or disagreements over what constitutes due process, or how pursuit of the guilty and protection of the innocent might occasionally result in deplorable, but regretfully unavoidable, miscarriages of justice.

But no one ever steps forward and says, "He deserved to be acquitted. He paid that judge good money for that decision." Or, "He comes from a good family you know. It is a terrible shame what he did to that poor girl, but he is going to pay for all of her medical bills, and college tuition too. It would just break his mother's heart if we sent him off to jail."

Some may argue we don't really achieve it, but nobody claims we shouldn't *require* Equality Under the Law.

In matters of tax policy, however, we don't even pretend to seek equal treatment.

Instead, our government has crafted a remarkably Byzantine structure of incentives and preferences: taxing revenues differently based upon their varying source and magnitude, using exclusions, deductions, multiple rate schedules, alternative minimum calculations, surcharges, phantom trust accounting, etc., etc. etc., ad infinitum – every imaginable form of sleight-of-hand, all designed to make the result indecipherable. Then, they hide behind the pretense that what they have done is "equitable".

I disagree. It's not equitable. It's duplicitous.

I'm not done with this topic. I will come back to it... with some specific suggestions. But I don't think I need to argue its importance too much more at this time.

For the time being, let me simply state that accepting equal responsibility regarding the civic and financial obligations each of us as citizens has to our society is comparable in importance to our right to equal treatment under the law. Unless we are all in the boat together, rich, poor, educated, illiterate, working class, leisure class and *political class*, all operating with shared obligations and benefits, our Democratic Republic is destined to consist of antagonistic factions, each seeking to pull the wool over the other's eyes so they can gain unfair advantage.

Another Caveat:

Please don't misconstrue the preceding commentary as another blind rant against affirmative action. There are indeed wrongs in society that need to be righted. There are historic penalties which have been imposed upon some that scream out for some measure of restitution or correction.

Certainly I urge caution regarding all preferences. I believe that it is dangerous to be too cavalier in either a) ignoring the obligations of society to find ways to target assistance and support toward the downtrodden and unfortunate, or b) viewing classes of people in a manner which reinforces and perpetuates their victimization.

But it is not toward affirmative action that my comments are aimed. My target is the preferences provided to the already privileged.

Once one begins to find purchase upon and ascend the ladder of affluence and status, political shelter for favored constituencies must be quashed.

3. AN INFORMED ELECTORATE

Honesty, integrity and judgment: these are the fundamental requirements we should impose upon our elected representatives. But we do ourselves and our society a disservice if we do not also extend those requirements to the public at large. We cannot and should not expect our representatives to act responsibly and honorably on our behalf if we don't become participants in the public dialogue regarding the issues.

I do of course anticipate some blowback on this point.

Some will simply laugh at the outrageous imbecility of suggesting that the electorate is interested in or willing to be informed. I laughed myself at a recent extended 11:00 PM rant by Jon Stewart on this topic. He used his Daily Show pulpit to chastise President Obama at some length for ignorance and naïveté in thinking that opinions at the fringe of his (Obama's) opposition could be influenced by "rational policy decisions and an even temperament". I cannot dispute Mr. Stewart's observation; opinions on the fringe are not going to be swayed by rational argument.

But it is nonetheless hard to dispute the need for an informed electorate to assist in providing guidance and direction to our representatives. Certainly better men than I have struggled with the question and the challenge.

> *"The best argument against democracy is a five-minute conversation with the average voter."*
> — Winston Churchill (1874-1965)

> *"I know no safe repository of the ultimate powers of society but the people themselves; and if we think them not enlightened enough to exercise their control with a wholesome discretion, the remedy is not to take it from them, but to inform their discretion by education."*
> — Thomas Jefferson (1743-1826)

Though I am sensitive to Churchill's observation, obviously I've sided with Jefferson on this matter. If not, I wouldn't have invested the effort required to put this book in your hands.

But how can we, as a society, make that happen?

We have to take our cue from Jefferson. We have to educate ourselves and our fellow citizens. We have to confront the delusional rationalizations and misrepresentations that have come to characterize our political debate.

We have to demand ...

4. HONESTY IN PUBLIC DISCOURSE

I know. I've already exceeded the seven citations required to reinforce my point on this topic. But my list of requirements cannot be complete if I leave this item off.

I will not expand aggressively on the examples already provided. But I don't think you can have items one through three above without demanding intellectually honest public debate.

Hopefully by now you are beginning to see my perspective. Perhaps you are even coming to share it.

Every time a political debate takes place with opposing parties talking past each other, citing irreconcilably conflicting facts, it does a little more damage to the foundation of our government.

"I can remember way back when a liberal was one who was generous with his own money."
— Will Rogers (1879-1935)

"Nobody spends somebody else's money as carefully as he spends his own. Nobody uses somebody else's resources as carefully as he uses his own."
— Milton Friedman (1912-2006)

CHAPTER 7

THE ROOT OF ALL EVIL

Is there any reader who doesn't believe they know the target of this chapter heading? You're almost right.

While some may not recognize the original source of the full quote, I suspect nearly everyone is familiar with the truncated adage that, "Money is the root of all evil".

In fact the source quote is a bit more pointed. Found in the King James Bible at Timothy 6:10, it was attributed to Jesus, that "the *love* of money is the root of all evil".

With no disrespect to the Bible intended, for my purposes I would shift perspective still further and observe that, in regard to the political process and workings of government, it is the use of *"Other People's Money"*, and most specifically the manner in which using Other People's Money affects our judgment, which I believe to be most damaging.

Money itself is the source of much good in the world. Access to it allows us to put food on the table and roofs over our heads to shelter us from the elements. As I write today, Americans and citizens of many other developed nations across the world community are once again displaying their personal charity and generosity by reaching into their wallets and sharing their resources with the residents of Haiti in the aftermath of a devastating earthquake. The success and accumulation of wealth among those developed nations is a fundamental prerequisite to that charity and generosity, without which it could not so readily be made available.

So money itself is not a problem, nor apparently is the desire (at least at normal levels) of most people to acquire money. Measured by most common standard-of-living indicators, the developed capitalist nations of the world, which respect and enforce property rights and encourage the accumulation of wealth, seem to be getting things more right than wrong.

> *"Economic development over the past two centuries has taken most of humanity from lives that were brutal, ignorant and short, to personal health and security, material comfort and knowledge that were unknown to the elites of the wealthiest and most powerful societies in earlier times."*
>
> — Ross Garnaut (1946-)

I see no need to spend time in this book citing the facts of the preceding observation, but if you doubt it to be true, I urge you to read Part II of Bjorn Lomborg's excellent book, *The Skeptical Environmentalist*. An Associate Professor of Statistics at the University of Aarhus in Denmark, Lomborg invests some 50 pages far better than I can in refuting the perception that the civilized world is going to hell and, along the way, he shows clearly that benefits of its improvement are broadly dispersed throughout all economic strata, top to bottom. Parts of his book can be a little dry and challenging, but if you're interested, it's a worthwhile read and provides a valuable a lesson in disciplined factual analysis and thought.

The conservative argument for laissez faire capitalism largely rests upon the following single observation: If the Alpha personalities engaged in the race to the top are dragging the rest of the world up in their wake, why shouldn't they be treated as Masters of the Universe?

The problem is when laissez faire capitalism isn't laissez faire. The problem is that people respond to incentives; and money is a very effective incentive. It is also often misused.

I agree with the Biblical quote, love of money can indeed lead people to act despicably.

But it is not just the love of money and the drive to obtain more of it that can distort people's judgment and values. The lack of respect for money, and for the hard, hopefully honest work required to obtain it, can be nearly as damaging to judgment as personal greed. It's not just evil that causes harm.

The only thing easier than spending other people's money is deluding yourself that when the Treasury prints more it's free – meaning you don't even have to take it away from anyone.

Financial incentives do have an impact. They may be good. They may be bad. They may work as designed. Or they may have very unintended consequences. Evil intent is a far less common source of damage than the unintended consequences of well-intentioned acts.

Here's a semantic observation to chew on: Surprises are often good, and consequence means nothing more than the result of an action. So why is it that when one refers to unintended consequences, it's always a bad outcome?

I think I'll give politicians a brief break and start with an example and some observations about the unintended consequences of manipulating financial incentives outside the governmental arena.

In or about 1973, when I was still an undergrad in college, I had an affection and affinity for the theatre. I spent a ten week term in New York City during which I saw twenty-four shows, a broad mixture of musicals and plays, mainly on Broadway. *Jesus Christ Superstar, That Championship Season, Sunshine Boys, Merchant of Venice, Pippin, A Little Night Music, Don Juan in Hell, Butley*, and more. It was a memorable season. I'm sure I never spent as much as $20.00 on an individual ticket.

It was the very first year for TKTS, the half-price, same-day purchase program established by the Theatre Development Fund. I thought the TKTS Booth was a great thing. It allowed this semi-starving college student access to the best of Broadway.

I almost never go to the theatre anymore. I don't think it's because I grew out of it. It's certainly not that it's inconvenient. And, although it hasn't always been the case in the intervening years, today, if I spot something I think I want to see, I can afford it.

But I don't often spot much coming to Broadway that catches my eye these days.

Looking back, I place a lot of the blame for that on the TKTS Booth. Following establishment of the TKTS operations, nominal ticket prices began to rise very rapidly. I attribute it (admittedly without a shred of disciplined factual analysis, due to lack of data) to an unfortunate interaction between TKTS half-price policy and the deductibility of business entertainment expenses. On one hand – if you're going to sell a large chunk of your tickets at only half their face value, what incentive is there to keep the face price reasonable? On the other hand – if you're using the tickets primarily to generate goodwill, the higher the price, the more goodwill – and with the purchasing business and Uncle Sam combining to pick up the tab, from the actual theatre-goers' perspective, "What's not to like?" There's not much pressure from either of these constituencies to subdue nominal price inflation then, is there?

Arguably then, the pricing impact was foreseeable; indeed it was probably desired.

But what other consequences might have been triggered?

- For the business entertainment audience, there's not a lot of goodwill gained by treating a client to a bad show, no matter how expensive the tickets. So the least price-sensitive customers aren't interested in a very broad product offering.
- For the regular theatre-going audience member, planning ahead and attending frequently both become more expensive. The producers and theatre owner may think they're maximizing their revenue, but at $130.00 per seat, adventuresome choices that don't quite thrill become a little more disappointing to the audience than they used to be. (On top of which there may be a mild psychological discomfort involved in wondering how much the guy next to you paid for his seat.)
- Advance bookings, particularly for adventuresome choices, begin to decline.
- Without reliable advance bookings, producers begin to get nervous. Standard fare starts to look iffy. They begin to trend toward flashy extravaganzas with something "special" to sell. They also turn sharply toward revivals with proven track records.
- Some cost conscious customers drift away, put off by the rising and tiered prices, and unwilling or unable to suffer the inconveniences built into the discount offerings.
- The TKTS customers, who apparently are more flexible and less discriminating about what they see, and therefore might support a broader range of offerings and maybe even have a more forgiving attitude toward variations in the experience, are viewed as opportunistic seat fillers. At least in matters of taste and product offering, they are largely ignored. No one designs their season around the half-price buyers.
- Struggling shows close quickly and never have a chance to "find an audience".
- Overall attendance declines.
- Offerings continue to narrow.

So now I'm no longer a regular theatre-goer, nominally because I've been disappointed by a couple of over-priced fiascos and I'm unimpressed by the variety of offerings set forth in the typical season. But the real cause is *"Unintended Consequences":* changes in the theatre industry which I believe flowed directly from a well-intentioned decision to implement a variable pricing structure in order to increase attendance and improve profits.

Remember, back in 1973 I thought TKTS was a great innovation. It is now my opinion that the Broadway theatre industry, its owners, authors, producers, performers, technicians, and audience all are worse off for the manipulation. I concede, it's just my opinion, my interpretation of an unscientific accumulation of perceptions and experiences over the years. I haven't made any concerted attempt to build a compelling factual case and I'm sure someone out there will be happy to argue the other side[25].

Note carefully: only a very small part of this initial example, the business entertainment segment, was related to the impact of using Other People's Money (for simplicity, I'm going to start referring to this as "OPM"). The knowledge that a certain segment of their audience was insulated from price sensitivity was probably a factor in the decision to establish the TKTS program but likely not the most compelling component. I deliberately chose this example to open this discussion, in part because the OPM factor, while present, is still very small. It was chosen primarily as an example of the hidden risks in the form of unintended consequences that often arise from well-intentioned manipulation attempts. The bulk of these unintended consequences arose simply from confusing the incentives and perceived value of the product offering, thereby, I believe, disrupting the stability of the core customer base.

As the temptation and opportunity to use OPM begins to grow the incentives become more warped and the consequences typically much more damaging.

Before I move back to politics, let me take one quick swipe at the airline industry. Anyone who was paying close attention to the discussion of Broadway, should notice that the variable pricing and yield manipulation techniques used on Broadway are similar to, in fact patterned after, practices utilized in the airline industry. Only the airlines do it on steroids and the OPM factor is much, much greater.

With that in mind, now ask yourself, is there any other industry in America which is so thoroughly reviled by its customers? Used car dealers come close, but I personally still put them in second place.

Why are the airlines so reviled? Perhaps it's because the perceived inequities in their product pricing leave all their customers feeling more used than satisfied.

The airline industry has cycled back and forth repeatedly through boom and bust, first over-investing, then writing-off investments, apparently unable to find a sound stable business model. Central to the model they do use is highly variable pricing, which imposes severe price penalties on their highly-valued business travelers (whose tickets are typically purchased with OPM), while providing essentially the same product at below cost to the more flexible but price-sensitive leisure traveler.

---

[25] A paper found on-line entitled Price Discrimination in Broadway Theatre, authored by Phillip Leslie at Stanford University, examines data from a single 1996 Broadway show and seems to conclude that price discrimination improves attendance while it maximizes revenue. But he makes no observations on the influence price discrimination had upon product offerings and the overall attendance, profitability and general health of the industry.

Then, in order to provide some justification for the pricing differential, they treat their customers like two (sometimes three) different classes of cattle, making sure that the coach customers are noticeably uncomfortable so the handful of lucky spendthrifts or frequent flyers in the front cabin can feel superior.

The alternative to this approach might be to plan and modify capacity and pricing into a better equilibrium – essentially acting like a normal business. If you can't make a fair profit at a price people are willing to pay, perhaps you should rethink your business model?

Perhaps airline management is reluctant to forego the psychic benefit they now receive from torturing their customers?

Back to Politics and OPM

From campaign fundraising to every appropriations bill they assess, at heart, every politician's job revolves around Other People's Money. It's unavoidable. So what?

There are two potential consequences which arise whenever one uses Other People's Money.

No. Strike that. Actually there are three. If you could suspend the laws of human psychology and behavior, expenditure decisions could be made entirely upon their merits and Milton Friedman would be proven to be wrong; OPM could be dispensed with the same amount of caution, thrift, care, and efficiency as if it had come directly from the spender's personal wallet.

But absent suspending those laws of human psychology and behavior, one of two alternative distorting forces is applied to the transaction.

1. If the source of the funding is voluntary, then when evaluating disbursements, the intentions of the funder receive special consideration and weight.

It seems obvious, doesn't it? If I provide you with the funds you need to get elected, it's quite likely that you will show some deference to my desires in the decisions you subsequently make. If you don't believe that the average politician has a big enough heart to show gratitude, then interpret it as political self-interest, and you'll arrive at the same answer. Voluntary contributors receive deference and influence.

2. If the source of the funding is involuntary, then the funder has no influence upon the disbursement decisions.

Well surely there's no distorting force from this, is there? Where's the problem? So long as you tax based upon laws, the source of the taxes has no undue influence on the use of the proceeds.

The wrinkle, of course, is when you impose taxes upon one class of citizen so you can provide benefits to a different class. This is particularly true if you actively use the vote of the benefit recipient to impose the tax for which he will have no liability.

As example: If I promise to add a $1 trillion health benefit commitment to the federal budget, while guaranteeing that I will not raise taxes a single dollar for anyone making less than $250,000 per year, am I proposing a rational and thoughtful tax and benefit program? Or am I bribing the electorate to participate in legalized theft?

I know, that's a bit harsh. But do you see my point? This is not a unique or particularly insightful observation on my part; it's the same insight expressed by Tocqueville in 1835. And by the way, telling a healthy twenty-five year old who's trying to get his financial feet on the ground that he has to pay as much as ten thousand dollars a year for health coverage he's decided he can forego may not technically be a tax, but it still takes money out of his pocket. Against his will.

> *"A government which robs Peter to pay Paul*
> *can always depend upon the support of Paul".*
> — George Bernard Shaw (1856-1950)

There simply is no way to get around the fact that our elected officials are placed in office to act on our behalf, and that requires them to make decisions about our money. It would be specious to simply complain about the fact that our politicians spend our tax dollars, since that is clearly a big part of their job. The core fact that they are responsible for both laying taxes and spending money cannot be avoided.

That said, it certainly would be better if our politicians were subject to the same impact as everyone else when they made those decisions, so our interests remained joint and common. If our elected representatives truly were Citizen Representatives, fully aware that a portion of every penny assessed in taxes and disbursed in expenditures would impact themselves and their neighbors ratably, we might be able to expect our government to exhibit somewhat more responsible and even-handed judgment. If the "laying of taxes" and the "distribution of benefits" could somehow be divorced from the electioneering process, we might obtain more responsible and even-handed judgment.

But that's not the way the game is played. That's how it should work. That's how we were taught in school that it did work. But it's not how it does work. Politics is a game of privilege, favors and power. Let's be blunt, it's become a game of commerce conducted through barely concealed bribes.

During Senate negotiations of the health care bill, Harry Reid and Ben Nelson negotiated a sweetheart deal for Nebraska without even enough awareness to be embarrassed by it. The fact the deal was later rescinded in response to public outrage doesn't change the fact that our leaders believed it was an acceptable way to do business.

Why are our tax codes and budget process so massive and complex? Because they are designed to hide what's in them. They are designed to create real and/or perceived advantages for fractional constituencies so that those advantages can be converted to money and/or votes. They are designed to move money from one person's pocket to another's.

It's not the kind of activity legislatures like to make too obvious. The surprise in the Reid / Nelson deal wasn't the fact of the deal, but the fact that they didn't even bother to hide it.

> *"The art of government consists in taking as much money as possible from one class of citizens and giving it to the other."*
> — Voltaire (1694-1778)

Voltaire wrote those words in 1764. He was talking about his times. A short decade later, Jefferson, Adams, Franklin, et al. drafted our Declaration of Independence and U.S. Constitution as their response and attempt to improve upon those times. They were intent upon crafting a better way.

But here we are today, mid-year 2010, with an American legislature that continues to treat the tax code like a carnival shell game: "Watch my hands… Where's the money?", as they rob from Peter to buy-off Paul.

OPM. It's everywhere. Every deduction and exclusion in our massive and ever-expanding tax code is a carefully (though too often inaccurately) targeted preference. Some will argue that they're targeted for social benefits, but I've become a cynic. I think they're targeted towards privilege, favors and power.

- Want to hide the true cost of employment taxes? Classify half as an employer contribution.

- Need support from Union members? The price is protection of tax deductible medical coverage.
- Need more premiums in the pool, but unable to raise taxes? Mandate coverage so the public pays and you can *pretend it's free of cost.*
- Can't get re-elected if you vote to raise taxes? Charge it to the deficit. Let the kids pick up the bill.

Sometimes it's not even real. It's just a perceptual bribe. Give deductions with one hand then take them back with the Alternative Minimum Tax.

Just like the carnival shell game, the objective is to keep the entire process so confusing nobody can tell what's going on. Look back at the charts on pages 59 and 60; with a minimum tax rate of 10% and "progressive" increases up to 35%, how is it that the average tax rate is only 12.8%? The answer is easy, it's deductions and exclusions. But *why* is it structured that way? Is it because it needs to be this complicated and confusing? Or is it a deliberate deceptive element of a one-sided game of chance? I have my opinion. I'll let you develop your own.

The worst of it is when, as with health care, the unintended consequence is markedly higher pricing and a dysfunctional system.

The fact that they were created with good intentions didn't stop tax deductible employer provided benefits from having a disastrous impact upon the development of our health care infrastructure. Our society would likely have been much better off if the medical care and insurance markets had developed differently. If medical care and insurance had developed as more of a personal responsibility and not become dependent upon employer provided plans, with the hidden government subsidy, it is likely that the disconnect between patient and payer might never have become so large. This disconnect is the foundation of dysfunction in our national health delivery process. It reduces patient awareness, interest and control in cost containment choices. There's little disagreement on this fact, which is why one of the most obvious and widely shared suggestions for health care reform is to eliminate the tax deductibility of medical benefits.

Yet politically, tax deductible employer-provided plans appear to be sacrosanct. Why? Because we're addicted to OPM. (Almost as though it were the drug that acronym sounds like.) Our politicians use it to structure promises and privileges to fragmented constituents. Unfortunately, in doing so, they inevitably also structure misplaced incentives and unintended consequences.

By the way, do you know how and why we managed to develop our heavy reliance on employer-provided health care? Government imposed wage controls implemented in WWII resulted in employers giving tax-deductible benefits rather than cash raises.[26]   Unintended Consequences of a well-intentioned government program strike again.

Even if it's just Mom and Dad sending a check on our anniversary so we can take our spouse out to a better restaurant than we might otherwise choose, most of us have some level of personal experience to guide our understanding of the impact of using OPM. So I don't think it will be too strongly contested when I state that in most cases where OPM is used, it leads to higher prices, though not necessarily the market dysfunction seen in health care. As examples:

- Business reimbursable expenses: We already touched on the two-tier airline pricing policies used to soak their business customers, but there is an entire class of restaurants and hotels that cater almost exclusively to business customers for the same reason: because they have so much less price sensitivity. I've frequented many of them. I'm guilty. I confess. Unless it's a big deal with my wife, when I'm operating on my own dime I typically stay and eat at cheaper establishments.

- The Mortgage Interest Deduction is one of the most broadly used itemized deductions, reportedly reducing federal tax revenues by $67 billion in 2008[27]. Its primary function is to decrease the after-tax cost of home mortgages, thus increasing the prices people can afford to pay for homes. Let's see, providing incentives for people to buy more expensive homes? How did that work out for us again?

Now I'm sure most members of Congress don't view themselves as robbing from Peter. They are not always acting solely, primarily, or even consciously for personal or professional benefit. There is legitimacy in their defense that they are targeting their actions in expectation not just of political advantage but in an attempt to obtain some social benefit.

Yet still I fear Unintended Consequences. Not just in the form of stimulating higher prices, but program outcomes as well. I've gone out of my way not to hide my bias. I am deeply suspicious of the hubris that says "We know what we're doing and can predict the outcomes." Experience says otherwise.

True believers in laissez faire capitalism, and I'm pretty closely aligned in that direction, abhor the perpetual government tinkering and manipulation that tilts the playing field and picks winners and losers. Opponents of laissez faire capitalism say it doesn't work, that it favors and perpetuates the moneyed classes. On one

[26] http://www.neurosurgical.com/medical_history_and_ethics/history/history_of_health_insurance.htm
[27] Comeback America, by David Walker, p 107

count those opponents are right; our system does favor the moneyed classes. But all that proves is that the system we have isn't laissez faire, because our government can't keep its hands off our wallets.

Every time they put their thumb on the scale, they shift incentives; and incentives make a difference. One of the strengths of human intellect is our individual flexibility and ingenuity. Typically as we complicate the rules, we open up new unanticipated avenues for people to scam the system. Good intentions notwithstanding, every time we consciously throw support in the direction of select, favored constituents, the potential to inflict unintended damages grows exponentially.

THE FINANCIAL MELTDOWN

Other people have written entire books analyzing perceived causes and implications of the recent financial meltdown. More people will certainly write more books on the topic. Still, I would be remiss if I were to close this chapter on Unintended Consequences, OPM and misguided incentives if I didn't point out at least briefly a couple of issues I perceive.

If you've already heard too much about the topic to be interested, I suggest you skip forward to page 122. I won't be insulted.

On the editorial side, there has been enormous consternation expressed over the magnitude and inequity of financial firm bonuses. Most of it has simply been slack-jawed astonishment at the size of the numbers. I will try to leave most of that for others to address and stick to a few topics, observations and points of perspective that I think have not been so widely disseminated.

1.   **"Why is Wall Street viewed as the highest calling to which our Best and Brightest flock?"**

It is an article of faith and a substantial component of the defense offered by the financial and regulatory players involved that "nobody saw it coming". The sometimes express but generally unspoken implication behind this defense is that the industry is populated by the Best and Brightest minds of our society. Why is that?

If you want to amass a fortune, you go to where the money is. If you want to attract talent, you wave money under its nose. The core attraction between Wall Street and our Best and Brightest is no more complex than that.

But there is a third symbiotic element required to support the arrangement. Why does Wall Street have all that money to wave? The third element is in Washington.

Back in Chapter 4, I commented very briefly upon the favorable tax treatment provided to investment earnings. I don't think it is accidental. There is a very strong affinity between money and power, and it is mutually self-supportive and reinforcing. Washington values what Wall Street has, what Wall Street does, and what Wall Street can provide. And vice versa. The favorable tax treatment and asset preservation policies supported by Washington make Wall Street's business model extremely lucrative. First, one shows gratitude; then, their counterpart reciprocates.

Certainly it doesn't hurt that many of them also went to the same schools together, belonged to common clubs, vacationed on the same beaches, and sailed on the same sounds. Mutual self-interest flourishes when placed in close proximity.

It is not my intention and would be unfair of me to suggest that the Best and Brightest among us have an outsized desire to amass a fortune. The desire to better our position is pretty universal across the spectrum of society. Money is both a means of easing the struggle of life and a way to keep score. Furthermore, money is not the only brass ring that the competitive Alpha personalities who drive innovation and progress and thus steer the path of society may be striving to attain. Some among the high achievers are more driven to seek power than fortune. Sometimes they go directly to Washington. Often they go to Wall Street and then to Washington.

The resulting relationship between Wall Street, Washington and the privileged graduates of our most revered academic institutions thus seems a bit too cozy and leaves many of us "outsiders" suspicious and cynical. This is not a good dynamic for either politics or the financial industry, both being arenas which most critical observers believe can best thrive in an atmosphere of trust and transparency. The countervailing and demoralizing view, of course, is that the "insiders" in both politics and the financial industry thrive precisely because what they do is not transparent and therefore they shouldn't be trusted.

Subjectively, one has to wonder if it may be possible that other industries, given the same political support and advantages as financial services, might become more profitable and thus more attractive to the Best and Brightest than they are the under current climate. Are the services provided by the financial industry truly of such benefit to society that they merit the favorable treatment they receive?

2.   "Is Trading in stocks and securities Investing? Speculating? Or Pure Gambling?"

The Wall Street community has proudly developed into what is clearly the highest paid concentration of professionals in the nation. (Top level professional athletes and entertainers probably think they have it good, but if one were to compare the breadth and depth of top ranks across their respective industries and incorporate career length and lifetime earnings, not just peak years, I would expect Wall Street to easily come out on top.)

Surely this must mean that these financial professionals are performing a high value-added service which justifies their compensation, right? Revisiting Lloyd Blankfein's defense of his industry cited earlier, the full published quote was, *"We're very important. We help companies to grow by helping them to raise capital. Companies that grow create wealth. This, in turn, allows people to have jobs that create more growth and more wealth. It's a virtuous cycle."*

That's the rationale for the stock exchanges, indeed for the entire financial services community; they capitalize our industries. That's the rationale they use for taking their slice, be it thin or not-so-thin, off the top of every financial transaction.

Now without wanting to prick too big a hole in their self-congratulatory bubble, I might offer just two simple observations:

First, the New York Stock Exchange's ("NTSE") website cites statistics showing that its aggregate market capitalization at the end of March 2010 was $13.4 trillion and their trailing twelve month trading volume as of March 2010 was $16.9 trillion. They don't report IPO proceeds for directly comparable periods but do list IPO proceeds in fiscal 2008 (before the markets tanked) of $26 billion, an amount equal to only 0.19% of its recent market cap and 0.15% of recent annual trading volume. To be clear, annual IPO proceeds, i.e. actual proceeds of investments into listed firms, were less than 0.2% of the NYSE's recent annual trading volume or current aggregate value. Only a fraction of that actually was destined to finance operations or growth, since offerings of that nature are often used to purchase private holdings.

Publicly traded shares do facilitate liquidity, allowing holders an ease of entry and exit and that does represent a benefit to investors and society. But let's not get crazy with the view that this is some sort of higher calling. I would remind people that every time a public share is traded, it does not represent a direct investment into the company. If one believes strongly in the efficient market theory, then every time an individual, bank, hedge fund or any person or entity, initiates a transaction they are adding to the global information base and participating in "properly" valuing the business. But I consider it a leap of faith to conclude that all that churning of ownership is doing a great deal to benefit society and the productive economy. I don't think I'm alone in questioning whether the services provided by the financial sector deserve the preferential treatment and honored position they receive.

Second, time after time studies of stock picking prowess have reaffirmed the finding that managed portfolios were not reliably more profitable than index funds or dart board picks. It is frequently alleged that, after fees, the majority of managed funds perform less favorably than comparable sector index funds.   This doesn't speak too well for the value-added function of professional stock-pickers.

Of course, I have seen dart players of such skill that perhaps betting upon them could be characterized as investing – so long as the Book didn't get to set variable odds and handicap their performance.   But if *randomly* throwing darts at the financial section of the Wall Street Journal can result in performance that equals most professional stock-pickers, one has to question the inflated value we place upon their services.

There is a reason why we describe trading stocks as *"playing the market"*.

3.   **"Are Wall Street Bonuses Justified?"**

This is clearly an eye-of-the-beholder question.

The typical hedge fund compensation formula is a fixed 1 ½ to 2 % management fee, plus 20% of investment profits. On a $3 billion hedge fund, and it's absolutely astounding how many of those are out there, that's $45 - $60 million to pay base salaries and run operations. Plus profits. In my experience, hedge funds tend to be streamlined operations; there is not a lot of bureaucratic feather-bedding going on. Most hedge fund employees are well paid even at their base compensation.

I know of at least one very successful hedge fund that takes a somewhat smaller management fee and a substantially higher profit percentage – but doesn't charge it on total profits, just the portion that exceeds a benchmark performance level. Confusing, but not a bad deal. They provide their investors with some downside protection, but when they perform well, they (the fund managers) are compensated even more highly than they would be through the more standard formula.

According to a news release in January 2010, in the recession year of 2009, Goldman Sachs paid $16.2 billion in compensation and benefits on net revenue (essentially income on services and investments) of $45.2 billion. At 35.8% of net revenue (down from 48% the prior year) it was reported to be the lowest ratio payout in the firm's history, ostensibly compressed in response to public outrage and embarrassment over such opulent compensation in the midst of double digit national unemployment.

So what does that mean? While it's hard to tell whether this 36%/48% payout at Goldman is higher or lower than their hedge fund counterparts, it's clear that the men and women who run our financial firms are paid exceedingly well. They are guaranteed large compensation in return for the chance to play the game and receive a very large portion of the profits even if they lose (or as they might describe it, the markets turn against them).

So what? Are they gouging their customers? Making too much money? Maybe. But that's pretty subjective and whose call is it anyway? Presumably they don't hold guns to their customer's heads and make them pay those exorbitant fees. Are their shareholders being fleeced? Maybe. But again, so what? Whose job is it to protect them? Shareholders are buried in disclosures. They're represented by Boards of Directors.   (How well, or poorly, is open to conjecture and debate, but that's the structure.) Unless the shareholders were defrauded, it's their own job to watch their investments. Other than curiosity or jealousy, why do I care?

If we, the government and other ought-to-be-disinterested third parties, believe the industry practices are unconscionable, we can try to shame them into reforming. Good luck with that.

If our government is treating these industries preferentially, thus distorting incentives and encouraging risky behavior and damaging consequences, *we should make our government stop encouraging undesirable behavior.* More on that later.

But for the record, the current populist urge to single them out for discriminatory and punitive fees and taxes is a remarkably bad and dangerous idea. We should eliminate the unwarranted preferences and unequal treatment they presently receive. But we should not try to punish them with unequal treatment.

4.   **"Should the Government have bailed out the financial wizards on Wall Street responsible for the collapse?"**

It's the wrong question, but stated as broadly as it is, the only correct answer is yes. Supporting the continuing operations of the financial industry was critical. They didn't spiral out of control, they didn't collapse; the Fed, the Treasury, the White House, and even the Congress deserve and should share credit for that.

5.   An important wrinkle upon question #4 is, "**Who did we bail out?**"

It is appropriate to recognize that much of the public usage of this term is at best imprecise, and often misleading. To illustrate:

AIG - The government "rescue" of AIG was not a "bailout of the *company*", it was a cram-down. The government stepped in and **bailed out AIG's contract holders**, after concluding that allowing all AIG's contracts to default would/could result in irreversible damage across the financial system. The government put in $85 billion in secured debt and seized 79.9% of the equity (via warrants). AIG's preexisting shareholders lost between 96%-98% of the value of their investment (including the pre-take-over stock decline).

Goldman Sachs – GS reportedly received some $20 billion in life-line loans which allowed it to weather the storm. But they were loans and they have now been paid back in full with interest. It was life-support. But it was not exactly a gift. On the other hand, the back-door benefit Goldman Sachs received when the government stepped in to honor AIG's credit-swap contracts and the zero interest loans provided by the FED to artificially inflate GS's profitability did look a lot like gifts.

Chrysler – Chrysler is not a financial firm but is worth addressing anyway. Chrysler was a bailout; why and for whom is not so straightforward. The government threw new money in, knowing in all likelihood it wouldn't come out (and it didn't). They made that decision in order to kick the can down the road a few months in hopes of avoiding a total collapse. The government twisted the arms of the secured lenders, forcing them to take a write-down of the debt while the assets and substantial value of the estate passed over the priorities to fund union pension liabilities while inducing Fiat to take control of the assets (essentially for free) to keep the business operating.   The government wrote off the $4 billion loan offered in December 2008 "to avoid bankruptcy", provided $7 billion of post-bankruptcy financing and delivered the post-bankruptcy NewCo Chrysler equity into the hands of the Union and Fiat.   Now *that's a Bail-Out!...* for the Union and employees. But it was a cram-down of the secured lenders. Note that I'm not saying it was a bad decision. Only time will tell whether resurrecting Chrysler from the dead results in a stronger or weaker U.S. auto market. Actually, we'll never know, because we'll never see the alternate path.

My point, of course, is that the imprecise and derogatory implications behind painting all government interventions equally as "bail-outs" are not helpful to illuminating either the broad scope of benefits or any potential longer term risks that did or will result from the government's responsive actions to the crisis.

6.   **A better question (better than #4 above) would be, "Did we get the best price for the support we provided?"**

Since I don't believe that we live in the best of all possible worlds, I have to conclude probably not. Certainly there could have been different structures used.

At roughly the same time the government put its $20 billion into Goldman Sachs, Warren Buffet put in $5 Billon. Mr. Buffet got better terms. Maybe the folks we rely on at Treasury and the Fed aren't as smart or aggressive as Mr. Buffett. Or maybe our government officials were looking at different priorities and objectives?

Fortunately, Treasury pretty much abandoned the original TARP proposal, which I thought would have been a disaster. Either we would have paid too much for the troubled assets, bailing out the holders by over-paying, or we would have imposed forced sales at distressed values (i.e. below intrinsic value).

The preferred stock and loan-w/warrant structures used were, in my view, clearly the best approach. If some opportunities may have existed to get better terms for taxpayers, the more important goals and "greater good" were accomplished. It allowed most of the industry to stabilize and find equilibrium.

Might there have been other requirements or incentives that should have been simultaneously imposed as part of the actions? Perhaps, but as previously described, I tend to be suspicious of the unintended consequences that follow behind too much command and control planning.

Is there something fundamentally suspect about a system in which Treasury is granted authority to use hundreds of billions of dollars for one purpose, and then changes its plan and uses the funds differently? I think so.

7.   **"What about the moral hazard issues?"**

Ah, there's the rub. It colors everything else. While recovery and support actions may have been pragmatically unavoidable, so far it's difficult to see that much has been done to improve the future risk profile in any meaningful way. Unfortunately, some of what had to be done may have made the situation worse, and it's not at all clear what actions could or should be taken as alternatives.

As example – Let's revisit the compensation issue:

Hindsight is always clearer, so now it is easy to see that, for at least several years, compensation in the industry was grossly excessive. That's not a moral or subjective judgment, but simply recognition that if contractual compensation was intended to be 48% of earnings, earnings and payouts were inflated by booking bad loans and soon-to-be-toxic paper. For argument's sake, let's pick a round number, say $400 billion (roughly half of the government's $787 billion TARP funds) and assume that represents losses on bad paper generated in the five year period ending 2008. (There is sound logic for believing the real number may be three times that amount, but many losses have been surreptitiously transferred to the public balance sheet and won't be realized for years.) At 48%, $400 billion in overstated profits converts to $192 billion of overstated compensation, nearly $40 billion per year.

When Goldman and its ilk were private and most of the financing they put in place was their *own* money, not OPM, the moderating influence of risk/reward was significantly better balanced. But the shift to public investment structures which allowed management to maintain and enhance their compensation structures while engaging in ever-higher risk bets with OPM was indeed a recipe for disaster.

The issue, of course, is what, if anything, should we do about it? By my rationale in #3 above (which I stand behind), I don't think the answer is imposing central management and oversight by the government. As a laissez faire capitalist I think government should strive to remove itself from a direct role in the process as much as possible. It should remove as many of the financial preferences in favor of these Masters of the Universe which now exist in the tax code but avoid the temptation to attempt command and control management involvement in operational oversight or compensation controls.

In terms of regulatory involvement, Congress should not attempt to act on behalf of shareholders, but should charge the SEC with responsibility for providing shareholders with stronger oversight tools to provide them (the shareholders) with the means and responsibility for influencing corporate governance. Shareholders need the ability to exert greater power to disrupt the cozy protections which the titans of industry now receive from their Boards.

8.   "Is there an Unnoticed Hazard that remains to be addressed?"

Credit Default Swaps and Other Derivatives. I presume I am not alone, but the single biggest surprise that I encountered from all the many revelations about the market melt-down, was that transactions called credit default swaps were being written as bets against securities one didn't have to own.

To the extent I had considered them at all, I had always believed they were what they sound like: a transfer of credit risk from one set of hands to another, essentially insurance against default. If I understand it accurately (and I'm still not 100% sure I do – mainly because it seems so illogical I keep thinking I must not grasp all the facts), the wrinkle was that rather than insuring securities you owned, one could simply enter into a contract payable in the event of some specified, generally unlikely, set of circumstances, typically a default on a traded security. Example: Buying a specified value contract that would be triggered to pay in the event that GE would default on some series of traded bonds.

These unregulated, poorly understood "risk protection" instruments and strategies were designed precisely for the purpose of removing the perception of risk from highly leveraged transactions. If one held a soundly rated guarantee, one didn't need to worry too much about the quality of the underlying assets, just the credit quality of the guarantor. When, as with AIG, the guarantor was a Government Sponsored Entity ("GSE") perceived to be backed with the full faith and credit of the U.S. Treasury, why worry?

It is my perception that on the brink of default, the government had very little alternative but to step in and avoid the debacle, if for no reason than the fact that the nominal value of the derivative bets (i.e. guarantees) was so much higher than the underlying securities. Unfortunately, in doing so, they probably increased the exposure.

Because of that resulting increase in moral hazard and future exposure, the underlying circumstance that required the government's intervention cannot be allowed to continue.

It is my opinion that these credit default swaps and the associated derivatives market need to be evaluated, regulated and perhaps substantially unwound. Current pressures seem to be centered around increasing "transparency" and requiring swaps and derivatives trading to be moved to public exchanges. But I'm not sure that's enough. We cannot and should not allow our financial markets to continue operating as gambling casinos, and we must remove the perception that government guarantees are standing by as insurance for bad decisions, whether they be construed as investments or bets.

I strongly believe that credit protection transactions should be treated as the insurance products that they are, and regulated accordingly. Sound principles should be applied as to balance sheet review and monitoring, including adequate reserve requirements to ensure the solvency of issuers. The GSE's currently providing government guarantees for such financial products should be unwound and removed from the market-place. The existing practice of placing and taking bets on the future performance of un-owned securities should be banned entirely.

As of this writing, the proposed congressional reforms show little sign of effectively addressing these structural problems which were such a large component of the 2008 financial melt-down.

"*Every man, as long as he does not violate the laws of justice, is left perfectly free to pursue his own interest his own way, and to bring both his industry and capital into competition with those of any other man or order of men.*"
— Adam Smith (1723-1790)

"*America is not a mere body of traders; it is a body of free men. Our greatness is built upon our freedom -- is moral, not material. We have a great ardor for gain; but we have a deep passion for the rights of man.*"
— Woodrow Wilson (1856-1924)

"*The inherent vice of capitalism is the unequal sharing of blessings. The inherent virtue of socialism is the equal sharing of miseries.*"
— Winston Churchill (1874-1965)

"*Capitalism justified itself and was adopted as an economic principle on the express grounds that it provides selfish motives for doing good, and that human beings will do nothing except for selfish motives.*"
— George Bernard Shaw (1856-1950)

"*We need a free economy not only for the renewed material prosperity it will bring, but because it is indispensible to individual freedom, human dignity and to a more just, more honest society*"
— Margaret Thatcher (1925-   )

CHAPTER 8

THE ROLE OF CAPITALISM

I observed previously that there is a common misconception that tends to define our American Democracy as synonymous with capitalism. Though understandable, it is a false and misleading perspective. Woodrow Wilson was correct. The defining element of America is not the money-making ethic observed by Tocqueville - it is the "deep passion for the rights of man", a passion that we need to take great care to protect.

Nevertheless, capitalism and liberty do have a natural affinity. The respect for property rights, the ability to accumulate and retain wealth as the fruit of one's own labor, the encouragement of each individual's right to pursue his own interests; all these key tenets of capitalism provide a mechanism through which each American citizen can endeavor to pursue his or her individual happiness. Capitalism both acts in support of liberty and requires liberty in order to flourish. Indeed, capitalism and liberty are two sides of the same coin. Capitalism refers to the economic forces and interactions which occur when individuals control their own choices, both bearing the risks and enjoying the benefits of those choices. Liberty is the principle of freedom which allows men such individual control – but the benefits of such liberty extend far beyond the economic realm.

I believe that those who perceive capitalism to be, by definition, an irrevocably ruthless and *exploitive* construct fail to understand the relationship between capitalism and liberty. It is ruthless, yes. But capitalism is only exploitive when its functions are corrupted.

True believers in capitalism, who understand the role liberty plays in unleashing the power of entrepreneurial vitality and economic growth, recognize that when the wealthy conspire (both among themselves and in conjunction with the governing class) to keep their foot upon the necks of the less fortunate and block access to the ladder of success, they are not engaging in capitalism – they are engaging in cronyism. Rational economic self interest need not and should not extend to encompass and forgive duplicitous, deceitful and exploitive practices. Self-interest is not a justification for illegal and/or abusive practices of cronyism.

But the argument against cronyism goes far beyond the simple issue of what is right and just or fair and equitable. Cronyism destroys the vitality and benefits of capitalism.

I believe Shaw overstates the case when he posits that "no man does *anything* except for selfish motives". However, the underlying truth of man's tendency toward selfish motives is indicative of the tension between cronyism and capitalism. When the wealthy and successful conspire to protect against the loss of their favored positions, they undermine the workings of the economic engine and the societal benefits of capitalism which were so highly praised by Adam Smith.

There is indeed a great and continuing tension between capitalism and cronyism; just as there is a tension between liberty and a second subversive force which threatens our individual and collective independence, a trend toward activist, interventionist government which some have dubbed the "Nanny State".

The Nanny State and cronyism are anathemas to both capitalism and liberty. One of the key, continuing challenges I see confronting the American government is the battle to resist these continuous tensions which strive to divert us from the fundamental objectives of our Union – Life, Liberty and the Pursuit of Happiness.

Liberty and opportunity are effectively synonymous. But they come at a price. With liberty, comes risk. Liberty means an opportunity for change. It means each individual can seek and choose his own path, restricted only by the caveat that he *"does no harm to others"*. But all change is not for the better. So, from the top of society to the bottom, there is a natural impulse to seek protection and advantage in the struggle – protection of the status quo, protection against a decline in fortune, or a "boost" to help one leap-frog past one's fellow strivers. But acting upon those desires for protection against risk or a helping hand requires limitations be placed upon our collective liberties because the goals of liberty and equal opportunity and the desires for safety, protection and advantage are mutually exclusive.

Every time we place our thumbs upon the scales, whether it be done to protect the mighty or the down-trodden, we restrict our collective and individual liberties.

Pure capitalism in action is Darwinian. It is ruthless in that it does not and should not protect the status quo. It measures and rewards activities strictly based upon that which is effective. It freely accumulates the vast quantity of individual desires, judgments, and priorities from across the populace, as each citizen pursues his own interests and weighs his own risks. It enables experimentation with broad options, and evaluates what works and what fails in real time. Capitalism facilitates an amorphous process of development and change; imagination, ambition and creative destruction continuously challenging the status quo.

Cronyism, that tilts the board in favor of the already privileged, destroys many of the benefits of that Darwinian struggle. It protects the established order even when that order is ineffective. It suppresses the rise of new ideas, new practices, new technologies, new priorities, new "winners" in that Darwinian struggle. The accumulation of capital, the aggregate benefits of prior successes, provides its own advantages and benefits. The already privileged holders of these benefits neither deserve nor need further advantages from cronyism.

The shift toward a Nanny State is dangerous for similar reasons. Even though its impulses may arise from a better place, a desire to improve the life of those being regulated, its restrictive impact upon society is nonetheless an anchor that weighs us down.

At heart, the urge to impose Nanny State controls upon the population arises from disrespect for others' choices. The hubris that drives either the governing class or an electoral majority to force its values and judgments upon the rest of the populace is at heart a disdain for their fellow citizens, distrust of their judgment and an infringement upon their liberties. It is government performed with a superior attitude, an imperial air. It is precisely the kind of over-reaching interference against which our founders took such great pains to provide Constitutional and structural legislative protections.

As examples: What business does the government have in imposing rules or regulations upon the intimate activities of consenting adults behind closed doors? On what authority does the federal government believe it is entitled to force a young and healthy individual to buy insurance he doesn't think he can afford? On what basis does the government think it should impose coverage requirements and fix pricing in a private contract between an individual and an insurance company? Or restrict interstate insurance contracts and competition?

In the first example, whether referring to unmarried individuals, polygamists, same-sex life-partners, or gay-bath habitués, neither the government nor the majority have any business whatsoever imposing their views. Consenting adults should have the liberty to make their own choices. This does not necessarily mean that local communities must treat them all equally. If a community wants to create laws that define marriage as a union between man and woman, designed to provide support and stability for child-rearing, and then wants to provide those unions with special tax treatment to encourage that objective, the local community should have that right. If a community wants to refrain from offering those same "marital rights" and incentives to same-sex partners – one might shake one's head and call that community narrow-minded – but the local community should probably have that right as well. (Inasmuch as granting "marital rights" is an affirmative community decision I am not convinced that it constitutes a real and appropriate individual civil right. I tend to believe that affirmatively encouraging stable child-rearing practices falls within a reasonable sphere of appropriate discretionary governmental activities. However, I also concede this is a grey area, which dances back and forth across the line of "equal treatment".)

But regardless of any "community values", criminalizing non-harmful consensual acts between adults is clearly an infringement on personal liberties – and an inappropriate and intrusive role for government.

Frankly, I would apply the same criteria to evaluating government intervention in recreational drug use. If drug use leads to external harm or criminal actions, such as driving while impaired, those subsequent actions should be prosecuted, as currently is the case with alcohol. But recreational drug use should not be criminalized on moral grounds – even if it may be harmful to the user. If someone wants to spend a portion of their life in a chemically induced alternate reality – *so long as he does no harm to others* – why should it be government's role to preclude that choice[28]? If members of society want to apply social pressure, ostracizing such disapproved activities, fine, let them. But the government should not be criminalizing non-harmful personal choices.

Moving to the second example (and the corollary questions which accompany it) we return back to the central question of the role of capitalism. On what authority does the federal government believe it is entitled to force a young and healthy individual to buy insurance he doesn't think he can afford? Surely the administration can field a variety of answers to this question, most of which include some level of pragmatic rationalization. They may claim simply that "everyone needs insurance" a determination divorced from individual cost benefit considerations that imposes the administration's judgment as superior to the individual's. They may claim that "when the individuals who currently have no policies and pay no premiums become sick or injured, they will receive free care, thus they are actually already insured – just not contributing to the costs". While I find this perspective a stretch, it is an interesting rationalization. But it still imposes governmental decision-making and prioritization upon the decisions of the populace.

Perhaps the most honest response is the one most seldom heard, "the young have to be pulled into the insurance pool and have to pay more today in premiums than they will use in services because the aged will always use more than they pay".

---

[28] I will avoid the temptation to make an extended digression into this Libertarian perspective, but while I recognize that drug abuse often ends in serious personal tragedies, I still end up asking myself why we allow criminalization of all recreational drug use to create a <u>societal</u> tragedy in the form of a violent and highly profitable criminal sub-culture and an unwinnable war against a portion of our own population.

To this I have to reiterate the observation made previously in Chapter 2. If we mandate coverage and eliminate risk based pricing, we are no longer talking about an insurance product, but a social policy.

We may indeed want and choose to initiate a national health service. But if we choose to do that we need to be honest and recognize that it is no longer an insurance program. We will be substantially disengaging medical care from the energy and influence of the private capitalist engine. If we choose to do that we will need to *change the way we think of think about delivering services and controlling costs*. If we want to implement a new social policy we should debate it, define it, create it, and *fund it with tax revenues*. We should not lie about what we are doing and impose another unfunded mandate upon the populace. We can't pretend that free market forces are going to provide efficiency and benefit if we don't allow the market to operate freely.

One of the reasons why it may be appropriate to consider such actions is that *we have already substantially disengaged medical care from the energy and influence of the private capitalist engine* – which is why we have such a serious cost escalation problem.

It is my observation that many of the challenges we currently face regarding the delivery of medical care and its out of control cost escalation result directly from mis-incentives previously imposed upon the market. Capitalism hasn't failed this market – it hasn't been allowed to function. Government has had its thumb upon the scale and has inadvertently encouraged the market to develop in a highly dysfunctional manner.

The underlying problem is so well-known that it hardly bears repeating: except relative to the uninsured, the buyer of medical services does not have any meaningful incentives to control the costs. In fact, whether we have already paid the premiums directly or have received the promise of medical coverage as an employment benefit, the natural instinct of the consumer is to "use as much as possible", thereby maximizing the benefit received. OPM strikes again; in this case it's insurance company money.

This is not a favorable dynamic. Remember, capitalism is an economic system which is supposed to accumulate individual personal decisions about self-interest. The forces of capitalism are happily at work today. Having divorced the user from any significant interest in cost control, the accumulated individual personal decisions of medical care consumers are doing exactly what they should be expected to do – they are driving costs rapidly higher.

If individuals were paying the bills, whether directly or by choosing or negotiating premiums and coverage, it is hard for me to believe that they wouldn't be applying the brakes to this cost escalation. But as the market is currently constructed, there should be no surprise that they are not. It is a classic example of what Garrett Hardin called the "tragedy of the commons"[29]. When individuals have unfettered access to commonly owned assets (in this case the insurance company funds aggregated by pooled premiums) it often results in individually rational decisions regarding self-interest which are collectively irrational.

Capitalism is only efficient if the risks of individual choices and actions remain linked with the rewards of those actions. When we disconnect the consumer of services from the payor, as we have done in the healthcare industry, or when we convert losses to the public coffers, while leaving profits in private hands, as we have done with the recent financial bailouts, we undermine the beneficial workings of capitalism. Converting private losses to the public coffers is a severely advanced form of cronyism which undercuts the efficient forces of capitalism just as surely as all other forms of OPM induce profligate spending.

Currently the incentives in the healthcare market are poorly aligned with the risks. Congress has just passed legislation that I believe will make those incentives worse instead of better. We are expanding coverage, promising seemingly unlimited services, while pretending we can simultaneously reduce costs.

If we are moving in this direction we probably *should* nationalize health care. At least it would realign the decision process to reestablish a potentially meaningful connection between the costs and benefits of medical choices. However, we shouldn't pretend that we can do that without rationing services. The choices are simpler than they seem. We cannot afford to do everything for everybody. Either we make collective communal decisions about rationing services, or we try to realign risk and reward to unleash the power of individual choices.

Once again, the point of the preceding discussion is not intended to guide or resolve this healthcare issue and debate, but simply to use it as an example of how capitalism does and does not function relative to our government and society.

Capitalism provides economic efficiency and benefit through the aggregate of rational individual decisions. But it only works when liberty and responsibility are simultaneously placed in the hands of the individual. Cronyism and the interventionist policies of the Nanny State both act to undercut the beneficial forces which capitalism can offer.

---

[29] See Filters Against Folly, by Garrett Hardin, © 1985.

"A wise and frugal Government, which shall restrain men from injuring one another, shall leave them otherwise free to regulate their own pursuits of industry and improvement, and shall not take from the mouth of labor the bread it has earned.

This is the sum of good government."
— Thomas Jefferson (1743-1826)

"It is the eternal struggle between these two principles - right and wrong. They are the two principles that have stood face to face from the beginning of time and will ever continue to struggle.

It is the same spirit that says, "You work and toil and earn bread, and I'll eat it.""
— Abraham Lincoln (1809-1865)

"The great trouble with you is that you refuse to be a demagogue. You will not submerge your principles in order to get reelected. You must learn that there are times when a man in public life is compelled to rise above his principles."
— Henry Ashurst (1874-1962)

CHAPTER 9

PRINCIPLES TO LIVE & GOVERN BY

Whether express or implicit, every society develops its own code of conduct – principles which guide behavior and define the expectations and obligations of its members. Though many of them are grounded in religious teachings, I would argue that, at their best, they transcend the strictures of individual religions to encompass "universal truths" of humanity, i.e. guidelines for action and interaction among society's members. We have expectations and obligations that, when met, allow large groups of people to live in close proximity with a minimum of friction. Certainly the explicit intent of the Declaration of Independence, the U.S. Constitution and the Bill of Rights was to do just that: to set forth in simple and direct terms the objectives and the form of government, and to carve out in explicit terms the rights of each individual citizen which the government was charged with maintaining and protecting.

It is astounding how short, clear, comprehensible and yet comprehensive those three documents are. In their original form they took up a scant six handwritten pages, yet they define the form and foundation of our Republic. The guiding principles and objectives of our government are distilled into little more than three key phrases, a mere forty-one words:

> "… certain inalienable rights…. Life, Liberty and the Pursuit of Happiness."
> "We the People…"
> "… in order to form a more perfect Union, establish Justice, insure domestic Tranquility, provide for the common defense, promote the general Welfare, and secure the Blessings of Liberty…"

Oddly enough, the more express society's rules of conduct have become, in the form of detailed and technical laws and regulations, the more it seems that individuals seek to avoid their obligations, seeking technical compliance with the law while avoiding the underlying integrity and intent of the principle.   It seems somehow that the more government aspires to actively manage society, the more complex its interactions with its citizens become and the farther it becomes removed from those simple guiding precepts.   Worse yet, government seems to become complicit with individuals in those efforts to find advantage.

As we either broaden or narrow our focus, we lose sight of the core principles that serve as the foundation of our society.   Without meaning to imply that anything I might describe could improve upon the elegance and simplicity of the three documents and forty-one words cited above, enumerated hereafter is a recap of key principles I believe we need to honor in order to achieve the goals set forth by our founders.

1.   Honesty

Enough said.   I've beaten this horse.   I hope it's not already dead.

When we lose respect for factual and intellectual honesty, we lose the ability to reason and apply sound judgment.

2.   Fair and Equal Treatment

The promise of government is a contract between society as a whole and its individual members.   There can and should be none more equal than others.   This promise of fair and equal treatment is not just applicable to appearances before the bench and judgment before the law.   It must be applicable to all functions of government.

3.   Right and Wrong

One does not have to be an active member of an organized religion to agree with Lincoln that the concepts of right and wrong are clear enough across the scope of society to act as core principles to guide social behavior.   Only the most obtuse (and psychopathic) among us dare refuse to acknowledge that human interaction requires us to treat each other with respect.   In its broadest sense, right and wrong are simply the prisms through which we view and judge actions, evaluating whether they infringe upon another individual's Life, Liberty or Pursuit of Happiness.

"If all men were just, there would still be some,
though not much, need of government"
— Abraham Lincoln (1809-1865)

Even the most confirmed atheists and evolutionists, disbelieving of creationism, intelligent design, a life hereafter, or a "greater purpose", cannot reasonably claim ignorance of the concepts of right and wrong as they apply to our interactions here in this life.

Society's laws and practices should, indeed *must*, be viewed and measured in the context of human right and wrong.

4.   Consistency

I've heard it said that "Consistency is the refuge of small minds."[30]   Actually I've said it myself; it's a flippant and useful retort when one is caught in an intellectually dishonest conflict of one's own competing opinions.   But in reality consistency does have its virtues.

I'm not referring to the false consistency of maintaining the status quo and fixed opinions, stubbornly unchanging despite all argument or fact, but rather to consistency in regard to the adherence and application of principle.   Ashurst was wrong.   If your principles are sound you *must* adhere to them.   But you also must question them, challenge them, use and learn from them, and be willing to discard them when they fail to withstand the challenges.

The consistency that comes from intellectual honesty and the even-handed application of sound principle, leads to a stability of government which allows society to flourish.   Government cannot be capricious.   When it is capricious its citizens find themselves pulled and tossed in competing directions, distracted and unbalanced by the changing landscape, unable to find their own equilibrium.

Nowhere is this more important than in tax and fiscal policy.   False, misdirected and/or changing incentives are anathema to economic stability.   Uncertainty imposes paralysis.   Reliable adherence to sound principles is a requirement of a stable and effective government.

When one's principles are fluid and changeable, situational, fashioned and re-fashioned at will to fit varying circumstances dependent upon one's desired effects, they are not principles at all.

---

[30] When I sought out its source I discovered it is an amalgam of Oscar Wilde, "Consistency is the last refuge of the unimaginative" and Ralph Waldo Emerson, "Foolish consistency is the hobgoblin of small minds".

5.   **Caution and Restraint**

Government cannot be all things to all people.   Over-reaching in well-intentioned pursuit of narrow goals exposes us time and again to the dangers of *Unintended Consequences*.

> *"That government is best which governs least"*
> — Henry David Thoreau (1817-1862)

Our founders quite rightfully cautioned in favor of a minimalist government. In Jefferson's words, "*... leave them otherwise free to regulate their own pursuits...*"

The design of America's government was based not just on the founders' experience with King George and fear of simply replacing the King by another over-reaching power, but more importantly, upon the premise that Liberty was one of man's *inalienable rights*, a right which could not be realized and delivered unless government could manage to stay out of the way.

> *"Liberty is the capacity to do anything that does no harm to others."*
> — The Declaration of the Rights of Man and the Citizen; France 1789

The passion for liberty that drove the founders was not simply a reaction to the oppression and control which previous governments had historically placed upon the populace, but also derived from the developing belief in Adam Smith's "invisible hand" of capitalism: the idea that when men had liberty to act in their own individual self-interest, it became a driver of growth and prosperity for all of society. Liberty was viewed to be almost synonymous with opportunity. Americans were expected to take responsibility for their lives and their actions. The federal government in America was not conceived to be a caretaker or provider for the citizenry, but intended to be an extension of the people themselves, performing a limited, minimalist role and protecting our collective and *individual* liberty.

As we move our government closer and closer toward an activist, caretaker role referred to previously as the "Nanny State", we are losing sight of this caution and restraint, and in doing so, losing some of the independence, self-reliance and entrepreneurial spirit which have served America so well for the last 234 years.

> *"The taxing power of the government must be used to provide revenues for legitimate purposes. It must not be used to regulate the economy or bring about social change. We've tried that, and surely we must be able to see it doesn't work."*
> —Ronald Reagan (1911-2004)

I recognize that quoting Ronald Reagan is a dangerous choice. He is a polarizing figure, viewed in reverent terms by a certain class of conservatives while demonized by their liberal counterparts for (among other things) having initiated the profligate policies that have caused debt to rise from 40% of GDP in 1981 to nearly 100% today. But I see enough truth and value in this quote as a statement of principle that I think it ought to be addressed.

First, let me point out that the policies implemented during the so-called Reagan Revolution, did not actually follow either of the two key points embedded in his quote above.

The Reagan tax cuts were *designed* to stimulate the economy and bring about social change by forcing fiscal discipline, in the form of spending cuts, upon the Congress.

Moreover, inasmuch as Reagan's administration and every single administration which followed in his wake has operated with a deficit, they have all failed to accomplish the task defined as a "must do" in sentence one.

But failure to follow his own advice doesn't negate the fact that these two key points contained in this quote should be viewed as rules to live by.

First, *we must provide revenues to fund the legitimate tasks of government.* We cannot defer those obligations and leave them as a burden to our children.

Second, we must restrain ourselves from the hubris that tempts us to use the tax code to dangerously tinker with the economy or initiate social change. When we put our thumbs on the scale and try to manipulate society we not only open the door to unleash unequal treatment and abuse, we impinge upon the liberty we should value most highly.

If asked to retract my previously cited Three Wishes and replace them with a single directive it would be simply to:

Exercise Fiscal and Legislative Caution and Restraint

The protection of our individual liberties is perhaps our government's greatest role and responsibility, and its focus upon those individual liberties is America's most unique and revered feature. I believe that the application of continued caution and restraint in the exercise of our government is a critical guiding principle which should not be lightly set aside.

PART IV

TWO MODEST PROPOSALS

"Cowardly politicians, members of Congress, and misrepresentatives of the masses."
— Eugene V. Debs (1855-1926)

"I have never seen more senators express discontent with their jobs. ... I think the major cause is that, deep down in our hearts, we have been accomplices to doing something terrible and unforgivable to this wonderful country. Deep down in our hearts, we know that we have bankrupted America and that we have given our children a legacy of bankruptcy. ...

We have defrauded our country to get ourselves elected."
— John C. Danforth (1936-   )

"Your representative owes you, not his industry only, but his judgment; and he betrays, instead of serving you, if he sacrifices it to your opinion."
— Edmund Burke (1729-1797)

CHAPTER 10

RETURN TO CITIZEN REPRESENTATIVES

When I embarked upon this project my goals were modest. Stimulated by concern for the rising deficit, the expanding scope of government and the questions triggered by John Kerry's financial disclosures and Warren Buffett's challenge discussed in Chapter 4, I intended to explore the questions and ideas developing in my mind about inequities in tax policy. It was my intuitive belief and perception that tax increases are inevitable, and that without some fundamental change of focus they also are impossible, since the pressures from the top and bottom strata of society for preferential treatment are conspiring to place too much of the tax burden unequally upon the working middle class. I expected to perform some factual review and analysis and summarize it in a short essay. I hoped to first test and document, and then share, my perspective in the hope of stimulating policy discussions about alternative approaches which might mitigate the inequities and obstacles I perceived.

However, every bit of analysis I performed and all the reading and research I undertook led me toward the same conclusion: while tax policy is an important issue, it is the political *process* which is the fundamental problem.

It was only after I began to document the facts that my vague discomfort with the intellectual dishonesty of public discourse began to give way to anger and dismay.

I did of course have an understanding that our media and political class were inclined to be careless with the truth; freely spinning facts and perceptions to make their points and fit their pre-conceptions and personal dogma rather than applying disciplined analysis to evaluate the changing world around them. But that's not so different from the world I work in every day. My career as a consultant and advisor to financially troubled businesses is built around dealing with myopia and denial – bringing fresh eyes to challenging situations and helping people open their eyes to changing circumstances so that they may evaluate alternatives. Indeed, it was my experience with fact-based analysis and belief in fact-based decision-making that made me think that I might have something useful to add to the discussion.

It was only after I began to unravel the threads of misinformation that I began to realize just how great the distortions of public discourse have become.

As an example, when I started, I did of course understand that the frequently cited statistic that nearly one-half of Americans now pay no federal taxes was a hyperbolic distortion of reality, created by pretending that Social Security contributions are not taxes. However, I did not recognize the magnitude of that distortion. I did not know that when you correct for that illusion and treat employment taxes as the charge against personal earnings which they really represent that *our tax code imposes its highest marginal tax burden on individuals with earned incomes between $33,950 per year and $106,800.* I had never focused upon the fact that the *working class bears twice the tax burden as the idle rich.* Nor that the *very wealthy pay less in support of their government and society (as a percent of assets) than the average American pays in fees on their IRA investments.*

For me, those were appalling and distressing discoveries: core pieces of information, critical to any public understanding and discussion about tax policy, that have been willfully and well disguised in order to shield them from public debate.

Of course, as soon as you start to look for them, you can find deliberate and gross deceptions used as the basis for political debate everywhere you turn. How else can you promise not to raise taxes on anyone making under $250,000, and then require them to buy something they've decided they can't afford? It may be good for society. It may be good for the individuals involved. But it's certainly not free. And it's certainly not honest to pretend that it is.

Our politicians are establishing law and policy and inciting class warfare based upon distorted and incomplete facts, willful misrepresentations and outright lies. It has become so systemically a part of our political landscape that it is no longer even surprising to us when we catch them at it.

The nature of our political process has become warped by our evolution into an adversarial two party system in which scoring points against the opposition in order to win and hold office has become a far greater priority among our political class than the quality of the government which they provide. Professional politicians are a curse. Regardless of any good intentions that draw them to seek office, the system we have developed, in which they must work, imposes grotesquely distorted and damaging incentives upon those who aspire to or hold political office in the United States.

We require them to buy their way into office. If they can't do it with their own money, they are forced to buy support by pledging fealty to narrow and fragmented constituencies composed of individual donors, party machines, PACS, Unions, and an assortment of other special interest groups. Litmus tests applied by single issue advocacy groups are aggressively used to pressure politicians to adhere to fixed positions. We turn them into pragmatic chameleons when what we need are principled representatives who share our broader interests and exercise careful judgment on our behalf. We need leaders who seek out and evaluate the facts in order to find common interests and mutual benefits and address the difficult challenges of our times. But the system we've developed with which to select them ensures that we cannot find what we need.

What are the options? Are the people who echo Churchill and say American Democracy is the worst option *except for all the others*, correct? Is this the best option available? Or might there be some modifications that could improve the process?

I recently had an energetic and animated dinner table conversation with a friend who argued that if we chose our Congress randomly from the telephone book we would get better government. It's not the first time I've heard the suggestion, but he argued it quite eloquently. Perhaps he was right? Perhaps a jury-like selection process *would* provide benefits?

> We could use a lottery, drawing from the tax-filing population to establish a pool of candidates. Draw a random slate of at least a dozen candidates for every office. Give each candidate a home camera, one administrative and one technical assistant and a FaceBook page with which to publish their positions and platforms. Limit the duration of elapsed time from lottery to election to no more than sixty days. Conduct one or more run-off elections at thirty day intervals until a candidate receives a majority vote. Voila! Citizen Representatives.
>
> Pay each of the candidates the equivalent of a year's salary for their two to four month candidacy and pay the winners double their previous salary during their term in elective office. (Make it subject to a moderately generous minimum/maximum pay scale.) Let incumbents run for a single subsequent term, joining the next group of lottery candidates on the slate. Encourage ex-officials to write books and memoirs but forbid them from lobbying following their term(s).

In less than a page I just outlined an alternative option which could allow us to fill the seats of Congress with responsible citizens unfettered by the allegiances of money politics.

It's hard for me to see how we could get worse government from a group of independents chosen through a program like that than we do under our current money-drenched influence-selling system populated by poll-watching professionals. After all, we let a "jury of our peers" be responsible for enforcing judgment before the law, including imposition of capital punishment. Why shouldn't representation provided by our peers be adequate for performing the functions of the legislative branch?

If I were given only two options – either maintain the current reliance upon professional influence-peddlers, or a lottery of citizens – I'd pick the lottery.

Obviously, there are obstacles to such an approach, the first and potentially most insurmountable being the self-interest of the existing political class. But personally I find a lottery has a certain elegant attraction, not the least of which is the idea that every election cycle would bring fresh eyes to bear on the challenges and problems of government. Yes, it would put less experienced representatives in office. But it would remove the taint of money and influence from every decision. I would frankly rather put my trust in my fellow citizen's open minded judgment, than have to worry about how much of their soul they had to sell in order to acquire the position. Currently our representatives must spend at least 70% of their time stumping for either money or votes. It's hard to imagine that we wouldn't receive better representation if they could spend all their time evaluating and addressing the challenges and problems of government.

On a more practical note, just as obviously, the lottery program outlined above does not represent the sole alternative to the status quo. There are less radical and fanciful alternatives which could be used to transition away from the misguided and misdirected incentives that exist today.

One obvious option is term limits. While I'm not opposed to term limits, I don't see them as a particularly promising avenue for real change. In the first place, there's been a lot of noise about them for a very long time with little real progress. While it appears that the public is generally in favor of term limits, most politicians are strongly opposed and more often than not, politicians have been able to block the imposition of limits. Even when limits exist they seem to be treated in a surprisingly flexible manner. In 2008, New York City's popular Mayor Michael Bloomberg successfully sought to have the law changed to allow him to run for a third term, despite only eight years prior having taken a strong position opposing then-mayor Rudolph Guiliani's attempt to do the same thing.

More importantly, it's the attitude and performance of officials in office that is the fundamental problem. Term limits might be helpful, but if our existing two-party money machine remains in place without constraint, it's not clear that accelerating the turnover of semi-interchangeable party cogs will make a lot of difference. The real obstacle to sound representative government is the misalignment of our representatives with the electorate. The allegiance and subservience of our representatives to the financial contributors and fractional constituencies that get them into office are a much bigger problem than the number of terms our representatives are allowed to serve.

That being the case, campaign finance reform is a far greater priority than term limits.

On January 20, 2010 the U.S. Supreme Court dealt a severe blow to the prospects for campaign finance reform when they overturned long-standing legislation banning corporations and Unions from using general treasury funds for electoral advocacy. I will save discussion of what the ruling itself means and how it limits and shapes the alternatives available to actually effect campaign finance reform until the final chapter. The following discussion ignores that new obstacle and focuses more narrowly on the need for finance reform and suggestions of how changes in the electioneering process might improve the operations of government.

If effective speech can only be exercised when it is accompanied by the expenditure of vast sums of money, then the average individual's rights of free speech are no more than a figment of our imagination[31]. Restating the observations made in Chapter 3, the right to free speech should not be a right to buy control of the conversation and drown out the voice of the opposition. Placing reasonable limits and controls on campaign finance contributions in order to reduce both the appearance and actuality of unfair influence is not an abrogation of speech.

It is imperative that we find a way to limit the existing linkage between effective electioneering and money. We have to quit denying the basic facts. Currently, our politicians buy and sell votes. They don't like it. They try to pretend it's not true. But it's a fact.

Politicians buy votes with massive advertising campaigns, firing concurrent and alternating barrages of media dollars back and forth. It is an orgy of money. During campaigns, our media focus as much on reports of fundraising comparisons

---

[31] For elaboration on this argument, see Appendix III on page 211, the author's unpublished letter to PBS NewsHour in response to its 1/20/10 report on the Supreme Court Ruling.

as they do on issues – and for good reason. The dollars matter as least as much as the ideas.

Politicians sell votes when they go hat in hand seeking contributions, promising policy support. It is a fact. It is an embarrassment. It is a travesty. I suspect it pains (most of) them emotionally to do it. But they do what is required.

If we could set aside our denial and be honest about these facts, who among us wouldn't agree that change is imperative? Unlinking the connection between our Representatives and the moneyed interests which allow them to obtain office is the first and most critical step required to get them to start acting like citizens.

Can it be done? I think it can. But it requires a shift in thinking. We have to facilitate *Free Speech*. We have to make elections about information and communication, not money. We have to make it easy for voices to be heard, and hard to drown them out.

In this 21st Century, communication no longer has to be either expensive or haphazard. Revisit the suggestions regarding lottery candidates cited earlier. A camera, a microphone, a technical assistant, an internet connection, a FaceBook page. The basic requirements for information distribution are remarkably cheap. So why do we let our elections be played out as competitive fundraising exercises?

Perhaps we should ban all paid political advertising?... to level the playing field? Why not? We ban cigarette advertising. We restrict liquor ads. Are political shout-downs carried out over the airwaves less dangerous than nicotine or alcohol?

Am I being facetious? A little bit. But I'm more serious than you might think. Public broadcast airwaves should be made readily available for political speech. Every candidate who accumulates enough citizen signatures to qualify to put his name on a ballot should simultaneously obtain access to publicly funded election communications forums. I am not suggesting that campaign finance reform be used to censor or restrict speech. I am advocating that we *facilitate* the exchange of political speech and separate it, and thus our candidates and elected officials, from the current forced allegiance to money.

I can conceive of an atmosphere in which a candidate who chooses to use private funds to initiate saturation advertising would be ostracized and shunned as dishonest and untrustworthy. It takes some imagination, but roll it around in your mind for a minute.... If free information distribution was readily available and the approved publicly funded forum for serious political debate, but someone chose instead to spend millions of dollars to force his message on you, wouldn't you question both his brains and integrity?

External advocacy can and should still exist – but direct campaign contributions and the financial demands placed upon candidates seeking public office need to be very severely curtailed. I am strongly in favor of advocacy groups of all kinds trying to educate politicians upon the merits or dangers of various public policy positions. I am vehemently opposed to the current structure which encourages political candidates to trade policy support for financial support. Unless the ties between financial support and public office and action are broken, our public officials cannot act as the Citizen Representatives they were intended to be.

"Only the little people pay taxes."
— Leona Helmsley (1920-2007)

"Anybody has a right to evade taxes if he can get away with it. No citizen has a moral obligation to assist in maintaining the government. If Congress insists on making stupid mistakes and passing foolish tax laws, millionaires should not be condemned if they take advantage of them."
— JP Morgan (1837-1913)

"The income tax has made more liars out of the American people than golf has."
— Will Rogers (1879-1935)

"Don't tax you, don't tax me, tax that fellow behind that tree."
—Russell B. Long (1918-2003)

"Behind the ostensible government sits enthroned an invisible government owing no allegiance and acknowledging no responsibility to the people."
—Theodore Roosevelt (1858-1919)

CHAPTER 11

THE 2% SOLUTION

The initial genesis of this book was a series of simple questions:

- Why do the vast bulk of Americans pay higher tax rates than John Kerry and Warren Buffett?
- Why are our federal tax revenues assessed against income rather than wealth?
- Don't the wealthy derive massive benefits from the stability of our society?
- Does our income-based tax system really provide the most fair and equitable allocation of the costs of society relative to the benefits?

As a matter of broad and ancient history, taxes have typically been assessed against assets. In commerce, early taxes often took the form of tolls, levies, customs duties, and simple extortion: sums extracted from merchants as they moved goods from one place to another, with the cost of the assessment added to the sale price at the destination. Assessments of this nature were sometimes imposed by local chieftains (or petty highwaymen) whose influence happened to span bottlenecks in trade routes. But rulers of kingdoms and empires could avail themselves of such tax opportunities as well, simply by controlling the borders and highways of their territory.

Of course, rulers of kingdoms and empires who weren't satisfied by simply taking a bit of tribute when commercial transactions required the transportation of goods had other recourse, the most noticeable and accessible being land. Wealth in the form of landownership was both visible and immovable. Throughout much of history, taxes on property ownership provided the primary source of government revenue.

There is a fairly obvious logic to this practice: if you need to collect money from someone, you probably ought to focus on the people who have some, and landowners tended to be prominent targets fulfilling this criteria. The approach is supported by the corollary fact that the people who have wealth generally have a vested interest in the stable functioning of society as a means of protecting it. In fairness, this shouldn't be construed as suggesting that only the rich bore the burden of taxes, since consistent with long standing trickle-down economic theory, the landowner in turn would often lay his own requirements upon the serfs, slaves or sharecroppers who actually worked the land.

But ignoring this trickle-down effect, over the broad course of history, visible and tangible assets have formed the primary base for government taxation.   So how and when did the historical focus on taxing assets shift so strongly toward taxing income?

Arguably taxes on property are in fact taxes on the income-producing potential of assets. This does not hold true for asset seizures, or plunder as the spoils of war, in which all or most wealth is simply confiscated. But confiscation of wealth without concern for the citizens' ability to replenish it truly is theft, not taxation. Many early empires used expansion, domination and theft as a means of funding their government operations. But, despite populist rhetoric that equates all taxation with theft, laying taxes to provide funding for the programs and benefits of government is a legitimate activity. Government requires a stable continuing source of revenue. While figures of authority may be tempted to engage in confiscatory practices, the art of taxation is maximizing proceeds over time, meaning that practices which destroy next year's revenue should be avoided whenever possible.

To the extent one's property consists of a chest full of gold coins, one can always impose a tax by taking a portion of the coins. But taking a fractional piece of individual real estate is neither practical nor desirable. So government takes a portion of the earnings potential of that real estate. Government only takes the property itself if the owner fails to pay his allocated assessment.

I would posit that it's only in the last roughly 150 years that government's reach for a piece of its populace's income has been substantially disconnected from the visible, immovable and therefore accessible stores of accumulated wealth held by the landowning elite. I also perceive that it's really only been in the second half of that period that the holders of accumulated wealth have begun to be more favorably treated by the tax man than their less fortunate fellow citizens.

An antipathy toward pretty much all kinds of taxes has been a part of the American psyche since the Revolution.

In the early years of the Union the scope of federal government services was strictly limited. The government relied exclusively upon commercial assessments;

excise taxes on distilled spirits, tobacco, sugar, and other selected products, were supplemented by import duties and various transactional fees to fund its operations. In the late 1790's, the federal government imposed its first direct taxes[32] on the owners of houses, land, slaves and estates. Following Thomas Jefferson's election in 1802 these direct taxes were repealed and the government reverted back to relying once again upon excise taxes and import duties. Interestingly, Jefferson was reputed to be intensely opposed to direct taxes assessed against wealth which, he argued, had the effect of imposing higher burdens on an individual versus his peers just because the individual or his ancestors had been more industrious and successful. Without questioning his stature as a giant among the founders, I suspect the fact that he was among the wealthy of his time may have colored his views on this matter.

To fund the War of 1812, excise taxes and customs duties were increased, and the issuance of Treasury notes was used to supplement those sources. In 1817, Congress *repealed all internal taxes* and for the next forty-four years funded its operations solely with high customs duties and proceeds from the sale of public lands.

The first time income taxes were assessed in the United States was in 1862 in order to fund the costs of the Civil War. A person earning from $600 to $10,000 paid a 3% tax rate. A 5% rate was paid on income in excess of $10,000. Following the end of the war the federal government's revenue requirements fell sharply and the income tax was repealed in 1874. The bulk of U.S. federal revenues reverted to excise taxes and customs and import duties.

The income tax made a brief reappearance in 1894 and 1895, before the Supreme Court upheld a charge that it was unconstitutional because it was not apportioned equally based upon the population of the States – one of the clauses that Jefferson reputedly held so dear. But as government's role and activities grew and related revenue requirements swelled, concern arose and debate began to expand about the regressive nature and economic disadvantages imposed by the increasing excise and customs assessments.

Half a century after its first appearance, in 1913, the 16th Amendment of the Constitution granted the Congress new flexibility and the income tax became the core source of future federal revenue. It constituted a deliberate decision to move away from regressive transactional taxes and incorporate a progressive rate schedule which would shift a higher portion of the burden of government to the more affluent segment of society.

---

[32] Source: US Treasury http://www.ustreas.gov/education/fact-sheets/taxes/ustax.shtml. Kind thanks to Treasury for the clear and simple historical summary which was relied upon to provide select elements of this brief factual recitation.

The initial rate schedule started at a mere 1% and rose to a modest maximum of 7% on incomes in excess of $500,000. Less than 1% of the population was subject to income tax at the time. By 1918, only five years later, escalating costs incurred by the United States' entry into World War I had driven the bottom rate to 6% and the top rate, applicable on incomes in excess of $1.5 million, to 77%. But still only 5% of the population was subject to the income tax.

For better or worse, over the last 100 years the scope of government services and the revenue required to support those services have both expanded radically. We have assumed social contracts with the infirm and aged and undertaken a role as world police. The appetite of both government and the populace to expand services has grown wildly. But the antipathy toward taxes has not abated. Whether one ascribes the disconnect between the public demand for services and distaste for taxes to intellectual dishonesty, incompetence, deliberate deceit or careless self-interest run amok, the result is the same: we are on an unsustainable path.

Our budget process has devolved into a highly dysfunctional system where disbursement decisions are made without regard to available revenue, and revenue generation decisions are designed by professional politicians who will not personally participate meaningfully in the funding. Congress structures tax policies to protect its favored constituents. Those who are financially able and inclined to buy access and protection by funding the grotesquely expensive political campaigns receive favorable consideration as do the carefully fragmented constituents who make up the political base of their candidate. In others words, Congress protects the rich while showering promises, sometimes accompanied by actual benefits, upon their targeted portion of the electorate. There are only two possible ways to sustain this model: either fund it on the back of the middle class, or run unsustainable deficits. Currently, we do both.

Is there a different and better course we should chart?

Let's revisit the intention of the income tax. As incomes and affluence grew and expanded, the need for revenue to support government services also grew. An income tax was initiated to broaden the base from which tax revenues were drawn and reduce the regressive nature of transactional and commercial assessments – which fell largely upon the less affluent. It was deliberately conceived to be progressive in nature, reflecting a shared belief that the more affluent among society both could and should pay more of the burden.

In concept it was also simple. It was intended to be both fair and equitable.

In practice it has become a snake-pit of manipulation and avoidance. Disdainful descriptions of the scope of the tax code have become a popular means of describing its growing incomprehensibility and inherent dysfunction. According to the U.S.

Printing Office[33] the combined code and regulations total 16,845 pages, making it 12.1 times the length of the 1,394 page edition of the Bible which resides on my son's bookshelf.

Over the past 75 years or so our political class has commenced using the tax code as a tool with which to both manipulate economic activity and construct political and economic interdependencies they deem critical to maintaining electoral majorities. They give with one hand. They take away with the other.

I don't know about you, but they frighten me with both their objectives.

First, I believe it is simply wrong to use the tax code to construct political allegiances. If you share my belief that fair and equal treatment is one of the core principles upon which government should be based, then the practice of buying political allegiance with favorable tax treatment must be stamped out.

Second, the strength of my belief in laissez-faire capitalism is only matched by my abhorrence for crony capitalism. Crony capitalism both offends my sensibilities of right and wrong and distorts the workings of the system upon which we rely. I don't think Congress (or anyone else, group or individual) is smart enough to manipulate economic activity without triggering untold havoc in the form of unintended consequences. If you doubt that, I ask you to simply look at the role that regulatory incentives and Federal Reserve interest rate policy had upon triggering the recent mortgage and financial industry bubble and collapse.

Once again, I do not wish to hide my prejudices. *I believe there is no worse evil of government than to engage in the process of picking economic winners and losers* – no matter how well intentioned. I also recognize that if a majority of others among society can come to share that opinion, we could seize from our politicians their most beloved tool for obtaining and holding office. It would change the nature and quality of our government. I believe for the better.

Our federal budget policies need to be honest in matching the cost of services provided with revenues available. Our revenue raising policies need to be simple, fair and equitable. Our politicians need to be focused upon these simple goals rather than electioneering.

The intended progressive nature of our federal tax code, a progressive intention which I believe most Americans affirmatively support, has become so irrevocably warped that it is effectively nonexistent. Even excluding the tax shelters and favorable capital gains treatment from which they also benefit, *the estimated 12% of income tax filers who report adjusted gross income in excess of $106,800 have a roughly 20% lower marginal tax burden than the nearly 40% of filers earning between $33,950 and $106,800.*

---

[33] Thank you and kudos to http://www.trygve.com/taxcode.html. Their site provides some highly entertaining quotes and allegations from a variety of sources in addition to the factual US Printing Office info cited here.

When we allow our politicians and economists to continue framing the discussion around how to further manipulate this broken structure by raising or lowering the rates or thresholds, we allow them to perpetuate the problem.

I perceive no real choice. Either we continue to keep our heads in the sand, continue to debase our currency, and continue to stumble blindly toward a foreseeable financial doomsday (which will eventually lead to default on the social contracts we have made with our citizens), or we step back and substantially restructure our tax base and incorporate a tax on assets.

I have a specific proposal: **We should combine and simplify our existing employment and income taxes into a single two-tiered income tax and supplement it with an annual 2% Tax on Assets.**

Eliminate the bulk of our manipulative and counter-productive tax code. Eliminate the crazy-quilt rat's-nest of deductions and exclusions used to conduct the shell game of tax deception, and make revenue collection subject to equal treatment.

Be honest about Social Security taxes. Quit pretending there's a Trust Fund and hiding behind that pretense to make the working middle class bear a higher tax rate than the wealthy. Maintain the existing roughly 15% tax burden from the first dollar of employment earnings, but stop the fiction of pretending it's a Social Security/Medicare Contribution and acknowledge that it is simply a part of the general income tax.

> Do not misinterpret this proposal. I am not advocating here any changes in the Social Security/Medicare benefits programs. I am not advocating privatization of Social Security. I am not advocating changes in Social Security pay-outs. Evaluation of the programs and modifications of some sort will undoubtedly have to be made at some point in the future. But that is true irrespective of how revenues are treated today or tomorrow. The only impact this proposal will have upon those future requirements is it should make them easier to address because it requires recognition of the underlying facts.
>
> I am proposing we acknowledge the facts and quit lying about the use of SS/Med revenues today and the source of benefit payments tomorrow. There are no Trust Assets. Social Security collections today are being utilized as general revenues. Benefits tomorrow will rely upon general revenues.

Add a 10% to 15% step-up somewhere in the vicinity of the existing $34,000 earnings threshold and make the resulting 25% to 30% maximum tax rate applicable to all employment earnings.

> The only special tax deduction I can support maintaining is a modest increment to the step-up threshold as exemption for dependents.

If all exclusions and deductions (except exemptions for dependents) are removed from the tax code there is no reason why this two-tier tax structure shouldn't replace all existing Federal Income Tax revenue while reducing maximum marginal earned income tax rates (inclusive of what are now defined as employment taxes) to this 25%-30% maximum threshold.

Remember, the blended overall income tax rate today is less than 13%. The blended rate on all incomes over $50,000 is roughly 15%. Eliminate the bulk of deductions and exclusions and you will broaden the base of taxable income. Uncapping the employment component of federal taxes will offset the lower nominal rates which create the current false illusion of progressivity. Yes, it will revoke the current rate reduction workers now get when they surpass the Social Security threshold… as it should. The result would be a massively simpler, less manipulative and revenue neutral-to-positive two-tier income tax structure.

Corporate income taxes, personal investment income taxes, estate and inheritance taxes and gift taxes should all be *repealed* and replaced with an annual 2% tax on net assets.

I found it difficult to determine how much of what is currently characterized as individual income tax is investment related. My best guess, formulated and expressed back on page 64 was that $800 billion of the total $1,060 billion in 2008 net tax collections was related to earned income, suggesting $260 billion was investment income taxes. Corporate income taxes were $301 billion, estate and gift taxes were $29 billion, suggesting a total somewhere in the range of $590 billion of taxes would be repealed.

Statistics released by the Federal Reserve reveal that the aggregate Balance Sheet Of Households And Nonprofit Organizations (average for 4 quarters) contained $71.8 trillion in assets. Two percent of those assets would yield replacement taxes of $1,436 billion – less the $590 billion repealed, a two percent asset tax would result in a net tax increase of $846 billion.

If we weren't already burning deficits of over a $1 trillion per year, a Two Percent Solution would not only create a more rational and equitable tax structure it could have funded a large tax cut for the working middle class. In fact for some, it would anyway, because the marginal tax rate that currently peaks at 40.3%

would drop to 25% or 30%. Because the change would be accompanied by the elimination of deductions, it is very difficult to forecast who would receive exactly what net benefit, but it would certainly result in far more equal treatment than exists under current law.

My Two Percent Solution might not immediately and magically balance the budget, but it certainly would take a big step toward fiscal responsibility.

In my imagination I can already hear the howls of rage emerging from Wall Street and the entire financial community. If my suggestion were to gain traction that rage would shift to pain. An $850 billion tax increase imposed on assets. The world as we know it might come crashing down around our ears.

Frankly, it intimidates me too. So if you can tell me where I went wrong and how we have an alternative, I'm all ears.

But let's review where we are. We are driving very rapidly down an unfinished road with our hands covering our eyes and ears to blot out all the warnings of peril. Our course is unsustainable. We know that. At present, we rely upon deficit spending practices that fuel inflation. Remember, 2% is no greater than the cost of many professional investment management services. I happen to think that the stability of our society and currency are worth the price.

Don't be mistaken. I share that ingrained American antipathy toward taxes. I would greatly prefer to balance the budget by cutting costs and controlling outlays. But it's not going to happen. From the disbursement side, the Reagan Revolution has proven to be a grotesque failure. Starving the government from revenues hasn't slowed the growth in expenditures. Until we fundamentally change the expectations and demands we place upon our political class, there will be no substantive change in government disbursement policies. I've made my proposals as to how to begin making that shift, but whether we accomplish that or not, unless we fundamentally redesign our entitlement structures, we are going to either have to raise taxes or face a collapse of the system.

Denial is not a plan.

Furthermore, even if we *did* balance the budget with expense cuts, based on the perspective I've gained over the last couple months while struggling with these issues, I'd *still* be demanding tax reform as a simple matter of equity. It is irrational that we claim to have a progressive tax system while the working middle class pays a higher percent of its income to the government than is paid by the wealthy and most privileged. Congress needs to take its heavy thumbs off the scales and its sticky fingers out of our pockets and level the playing field.

What would it mean?

The two percent asset assessment I've suggested means that any year in which I earn less on my assets than two percent my net worth declines. If I place $1 million dollars under my mattress and it generates no earnings, and I take my two percent tax obligation out from under the mattress every year to give it to the government, at the end of 34 years, almost half my money will be gone. I will be down to $503,000. There will be some who claim that taxing wealth is highway robbery. As robberies go, 49.7% over 34 years is pretty inefficient.

Let's compare that to inflation, which we were discussing earlier. What happens to our accumulated wealth today? I used the current dollar adjustment data for the years 1929 through 2009 provided by the OMB in conjunction with their budget disclosures and took a look at what historical inflation has done to money similarly parked under a mattress. The first available 34 year period ended in 1963, at which point one 1929 dollar had declined in value to 55 cents. From '29 to '63 the impact of inflation extracted very nearly the same value from under that theoretical mattress as would have been assessed by an annual 2% asset tax.

That first available data point was the highest trailing 34 year value retention of the sample. Despite what we say or think about government's responsibility to protect the value of our currency, its decline has been inexorable. By decade, here are the averages:

Value Retention of One U.S. Dollar Value After 34 Years Average by Decade	
1970's	$ .30
1980's	.25
1990's	.23
2000's	.26

So... assuming our current profligate policies *don't* accelerate inflation, based on the last two decades' results, if I put a million dollars under my mattress today, thirty-four years from now I should expect to have between $230,000 and $260,000 of value left. If our policies today and tomorrow result in rising inflation, I'll have a lot less.

On the other hand, if imposing a 2% Asset Tax resulted in a stable currency, I'd have the full $503,000 referred to previously and be between $243,000 and $273,000 better off. If it cut inflation by half, I'd still be even... the 2% tax payments would effectively be wholly offset by the reduced inflation rate.

The cost of inflation is much, much higher than most of us realize in our day to day ponderings. Consequently, the tradeoff between higher taxes on wealth and a more stable currency is a far more compelling argument than most of us intuitively recognize. Stable currency policies are worth the investment.

> Reminder: The preceding analysis theorizes about un-invested "assets under the mattress". A mere two percent investment return maintains stable principal values. Returns in excess of two percent result in continuing accumulation of wealth.
>
> The long-term costs of inflation, which have been highly exacerbated by the government's deficit spending practices, exceed the two percent annual cost of this proposal – which is aimed at stemming that inflationary pressure.

Obviously, the issues and arguments, pros and cons, of an asset assessment extend in many more directions than just to inflation of the currency.

First and foremost, I would expect this proposal to be characterized by many as a discriminatory attack on wealth and the financial industry. It's not. As previously acknowledged, I aspire to be wealthy. By some measures, I already am.

I am not arguing that we should penalize the wealthy. But I have been questioning why we currently give them so many advantages and have found no justification for it. I do not wish to place capital at a disadvantage. But I think the advantage it currently holds is unjustifiable and the source of many detrimental consequences.

I overstate my case when I say I've found no justification for current policies. We have formulated a justification for our favorable treatment of capital, though I increasingly perceive it as more the product of rationalization than logic. We have convinced ourselves that when a man invests his capital, he is performing a public service: he is feeding the economy, stimulating growth, creating jobs – and *we think we need to give him special incentives to induce him to do that.* I'm sorry, but that doesn't conform very closely to my understanding of the underlying theories of capitalism. I thought men invested their energies and assets with an eye sharply focused upon their own personal self-interest. Mutual benefit to society obtained by the aggregate of each individual's pursuit of self-interest: Isn't that the core concept of capitalist theory?

Do we think that if we apply a constant nominal tax assessment against assets the wealthy will suddenly stop investing their money and shove it under a mattress? I don't. I think they will continue to perceive incentives to invest it wisely and make sure it grows. In fact I think a stable and consistent assessment of this nature will provide far more balanced and productive investment incentives than the capital gains and corporate earnings taxes presently in effect, which often incent both business and investment decisions to be made in consideration of tax avoidance strategies rather than more fundamental business goals.

One of the concepts I frequently utilize in evaluating troubled businesses is the idea of measuring the performance of investments in comparison to alternative "highest and best use" capital reallocations – typically measured by return on assets aggregating both income and appreciation. More simply stated, a business should be evaluated not only relative to its standalone performance, but with regard to available alternative options. If a business has a current value of $1 million, but the anticipated future return is negative or nominal, say 3% annually, does it make sense to hold the investment, or to sell it and redeploy the capital somewhere else which offers a higher return? Capitalist theory posits that the ease with which capital can be reallocated is one of the drivers of growth and economic resilience. Yet many of our current tax practices seem to run counter to the fundamentals of this and other components of capitalist theory.

We tax earnings that emanate from the transactions involved in reallocating capital, thus arguably discouraging such reallocations. We make long-term holdings fully exempt from our tax base – a departure from centuries of historical practice. We tax, thus punishing, profitable businesses while their less efficient and productive competitors bear a lighter burden.

My proposal eliminates the "tax-free compounding advantage" currently provided to long-term investments. It does not eliminate the benefits of capital accumulation, but it does impose a disincentive toward non-productive allocations of capital and provide a positive incentive toward the most profitable allocation of assets.

Current U.S. tax policies strongly favor investment earnings over labor.

Using the current tax rate schedules and ignoring deductions and exclusions, a person who works with his back, or his hands, or his brains, for sixty hours a week and earns $75,000 per year (employer gross cost) pays $25,080 in federal taxes (including employer portion of SS/Med), 33.4% of his employer gross cost income.   An "investor" who watches his shareholdings appreciate by $75,000 over the course of the year, but who doesn't sell those holdings, pays zero tax.

Were the same investor to sell those holdings generating capital gains (assuming they constitute his entire income for the year), his tax liability would be either $14,938 or $11,250, depending upon whether they were sold more or less than 365 days after their original purchase.

Capital gains earnings receive a tax discount of 40% to 45% versus wages and salary. A person who simply holds his accumulating wealth (the lucky soul already at the top of the pile for whom it is excess income, unnecessary to sustain his day to day existence) receives a 100% tax discount.

Tax Burden on $75,000 Income From Alternative Income Sources			
Income source	Total Tax Burden	Percent of Income	Discount vs. Tax on Labor
Wages or Salary(1)	$25,080	33.4 %	n/a
Investment Returns			
- Short Term Capital- Gain (2)	14,938	19.9 %	40 %
- Long-term Capital Gain	11,250	15.0 %	45 %
- Unrealized profit	0	0 %	100 %

(1) On Employer gross cost of $75,000, employee's nominal annual wages or salary would be $69,670.
(2) Short term capital gains are taxed as ordinary income, thus short term capital gains tax rates will move higher as income rises. But it is never subject to employment taxes.

While I anticipate the financial investment community will scream about the inequity of government assessments against wealth, today that community itself assesses significant burdens on the management of capital in the form of fees, expenses and profit participations. Meanwhile, many of the management services they provide are focused at least as carefully upon engineering tax avoidance strategies as enhancing real underlying operational investment returns. In this climate, value and risk manipulation in the form of exotic new derivative instruments and trading strategies have become the engine driving massive wealth creation and transfer. While the profits and underlying wealth attributed to these activities may indeed be massive, arguably, they are also often illusory. The financial industry creates valuation bubbles, from which they take their slice. Government policies are encouraging and propping up these illusory activities.

Without meaning to be too dismissive of financial engineering strategies which create wealth by inflating valuation assumptions, why should we think those services comprise such value to society that they should be incented more enthusiastically than labor? If the owners of capital want to shower money on people who inflate and deflate asset bubbles, who I am to say stop? But why should government and society encourage and subsidize those activities?

I for one find it hard to believe that the benefits of a stable society and a stable currency don't merit receiving a higher level and more equitable share of support from the moneyed classes than they currently receive.

PART V

OBSTACLES & OBJECTIONS?

"Every new idea starts out as an unimaginable and clearly unworkable challenge to the status quo."

— The Author[34]

"Status quo, you know, is Latin for 'the mess we're in'."

— Ronald Reagan (1911-2004)

"For every problem there is a solution which is simple, clean and wrong."

— H. L. Mencken (1880-1956)

---

[34] I'm sure others have already said this, no doubt more eloquently, but I don't know who.

CHAPTER 12

SELF-INTEREST RUN AMOK VS EQUAL TREATMENT

My objective throughout the preceding has been to illuminate issues, questions, perspectives and challenges facing America over the next decade in an attempt to identify alternatives, stimulate discussion and ultimately change certain elements of the status quo.

As always, when proposing changes to the status quo, the first line of objections arises from three simple questions:

1. What's wrong with what we have today?
2. What's in it for me?
3. How can this new plan go wrong?

The Status Quo

Clearly there will be some people who believe there's nothing wrong with where we are today. It's hard for me to imagine how, but it may be a majority. Nevertheless, I may be tilting at windmills that few others see.

I've described what I see.

We have a federal revenue and disbursement system that is unbalanced and "unsustainable"; that's not my word, it's the assessment of the CBO. We have created and are expanding entitlements to our citizens with near-total disregard to the necessity or our ability to fund them. We treat federal money as if it is free and limitless.

As a result, despite Americans' deep seated antipathy toward taxes, tax increases have become inevitable. Not minor tax increases. Major tax increases. The longer we put them off the more painful they will be. But a large majority of our leadership and populace appear to be in deep denial regarding this inevitability.

I started this review process with the simple intention of addressing areas where I believe tax reform could make those future tax increases more fair and equitable and therefore less painful.

But as I focused my attention on the tax issue, I began to perceive that dysfunctional tax policies are not the cause of our problems. Our structural budget deficits arise from deeper and more difficult problems in the status quo.

I perceive and believe that the fundamental core values of American Democracy, the "character of our country" which I believe was the source our growth and power over the last two hundred years, is being eroded.

Our political class is being corrupted by the system in which we force them to work. They have become isolated and distinct from the population they are intended to serve. They spend the bulk of their time begging for money in pursuit of power. They buy votes and support by distributing favors.

The process is corrupting us as well as them.

President Obama described our uniquely American character as "our self-reliance: our rugged individualism, our fierce defense of freedom, and our healthy skepticism of government". Yet I believe both our recent history and current path are accelerating the erosion of those key and critical qualities.

In Chapter Nine I described the prism through which I try to view the world, a prism of simple core principles:

- Honesty
- Fair and Equitable Treatment
- A Sense of Right and Wrong
- Consistency – in the form of intellectual honesty and the even-handed application of these principles.
- Caution and Restraint

It is a prism and perspective I try to apply to all things, not just the ideas, alternatives and suggestions which I have set forth as potential change, but first and foremost to the status quo. Does what we have meet these simple criteria? I think not.

It is on that basis that I have set forth on my search for change and a better way.

Self-Interest

When and how did unfettered personal self-interest become respectable? When and how was greed elevated to a virtue?

I suspect many observers, perhaps most, would blame Adam Smith and the rise of capitalism. As quoted previously, George Bernard Shaw described capitalism justifying itself by "providing selfish motives for doing good" – a skewed view which equates self-interest directly with good. But clearly *all* self-interest is not good. Adam Smith tempered his call for self-interest with the caveat "*as long as he does not violate the laws of justice*". The Declaration of the Rights of Man stated the same caveat differently, limiting liberty to actions which "*do no harm to others*". Yet today we seem to have forgotten these caveats.

The question, "What's in it for me?" should not be a limiting obstacle for every act of government. Self-interest *must* be tempered with a view to society, not just the individual.

The entire history of developing civilization revolves around the give and take between self-interest and the collective community. Many (pessimists perhaps) claim that the history of civilization is nothing other than an extended tale of elites exploiting the under-classes – starting with the first chief of a hunter-gathering tribe who sat in the village and waited for the rest of his clan to bring back the spoils of the day and lay the choicest bits at his feet. Others, myself included, see civilization (with a perspective which may be more optimistic than accurate) as a collective and cooperative effort to improve the quality of life for ourselves and our community. Yes, the driver for that effort starts with the individual. Yes, the pursuit of happiness is local, personal, and specific to each individual. But it is not, and must not become, entirely egocentric.

The unquestioning worship of individual, short-term self-interest is not a viable and sustainable ethic. Civilization craves more. We look to our communities and to our future: our wives and husbands, our children and parents, our friends and neighbors. The perspective that the greatest meaning of life lies outside oneself is a common thread that runs through all the major religions of the world. Personal self-interest – without regard to the rights of others or the collective good – should not be the guiding precept for every decision. When we corrupt the concepts of capitalism and liberty we undermine the strength of our union. We corrupt those concepts when we allow our government to engage in cronyism, playing favorites and protecting elites and allies. But we also corrupt those concepts when we impose Nanny State judgments and controls upon society and usurp individual choices and judgment. Good intentions are not an adequate excuse for the infringement of our liberties.

The founders of our union clearly foresaw the dangers of both concentrated power and a Democracy in which a simple majority could trample upon the rights of their neighbors. When our governing class believes their role in every governmental act is to craft a majority coalition of personal best interests, they are not guiding us toward a stable and flourishing society; they are setting up a competition of winners and losers.

The goal of government is not to seek *what is best for most of us*, but what is *right and fair for all of us*. The urge to seek and protect one's personal self-interest is a real force to be considered and respected. But it should not be viewed as a driving theological principle or precept of government.

Unintended Consequences

In Chapters 3 and 4 I set forth my Magic Lamp list, a compilation of three wishes designed to affect a better world and future. It's a common speculative pastime for people, setting out their priorities for change – a "what-if fantasy" of fairy tale wishes. However, it is dangerous to forget that the underlying fairy tale legends from which this pastime springs are cautionary tales warning about unintended consequences and the risks of getting what one asks for.

With that in mind, as someone who claims a healthy respect for, and fear of, unintended consequences, how can I be so arrogant as to sit in my office and redesign the U.S. Federal Income Tax system without fear that I am inviting economic collapse?... without even a degree in Economics?

I can't. But my fear of the impending economic collapse that must inevitably flow from our current profligate practices has argued strenuously that I fight the forces of inertia.

It is not hubris which has driven me to address this question, but a genuine concern that the judgment of the OMB is correct – *"We are on an Unsustainable Path"*.

If the status quo is not an option, as I have concluded, then change of some sort is imperative. The book you have in your hands is the culmination of my personal struggles with that challenge. It is my attempt to broaden perspective, open discussion and urge action. This is a discussion and debate that is critical if we are to either energize our leaders to seek real change, or have a reasonable opportunity of finding a better road.

Is a Two Percent Asset Tax Really a Viable Option?

If there's a flaw in the logic, I don't yet see it. That's why I'm publishing this book. I want people to explore that question. If you see a flaw, tell me about it. I want to hear.

Certainly there will be objections. They will start with self-interest and inertia. We've now accumulated nearly 100 years of history with the "progressive" Federal Income Tax and the continuously reinforced bias, mantra really, that governmental preferences toward investment income are the key to stimulating the economy. The academic and political classes are heavily invested in these ideas. So are the privileged and influential. (Sorry, once again, I'm being redundant. The academic and political classes *are* privileged and influential.)

But, thus far, the concept of a Two Percent Asset Tax has passed every aspect of my Five Principle test.

Honesty: I've made every attempt to be honest and objective in my factual review and assessments. If I've made errors or omissions I apologize; they've been unintentional. Having wrestled with this question until I think I've found a better way, I am now seeking to air my ideas before a broader and critical audience to identify if and where I may have gone wrong in my thinking. I genuinely welcome and desire the benefit of disciplined critical challenge.

Attacking my criteria of "honesty" from a different perspective, I believe the concept of combining a simplified Two-Tiered Income Tax with a Two Percent Asset Tax is inherently far more honest than our current system because it removes the incentives to manipulate and distort deductions, income and profits.   It eliminates the transparent fiction that we maintain a SS/Med Trust Fund and would remove most of the current incentives and mechanisms for governmental favoritism. Obviously there are still going to be people who will seek to hide assets and there will likely to be many grey areas of valuation which will require some level of monitoring, regulation and dispute. But, as conceived, it is conducive to honest and even-handed application.

Fair and Equitable: As noted at the outset, fair and equitable are highly subjective concepts – almost invitations to heated debate. But the consistent even-handed application of constant rates of taxation applied broadly to both income and assets seems to me to fit the bill rather nicely. In implementation, I anticipate and would propose a liberal minimum threshold exclusion be applied before assessment of an asset tax. But at a modest two percent, the reason for applying such a minimum threshold reflects expedience and practicality more than principle.   So long as politicians can be precluded from buying and selling allegiances by creating multiple excluded asset classes, it would be hard to argue that a constant two percent tax rate wouldn't be fair and equitable.

Right and Wrong: There are those who claim that taxing wealth is simply wrong. I don't see it. They argue that asset and investment taxes are somehow double assessments: taxes laid a second time on wealth that was previously taxed as income. I consider it a specious argument. We already currently tax real estate – as we should. Historically, wealth was a greater target for taxation than income. The sheltering of wealth from assessments for the cost of government is a fairly recent development which I believe is itself wrong.

A man of wealth and a man of labor both receive benefits from society. If a man labors and generates income, but has no wealth, he still is taxed – though his expenses may consume his income leaving him limited ability to pay. If another man has wealth, even great wealth, but manages it to avoid income, he is currently shielded from taxes – even if he has a far greater ability to pay. Where is the right and wrong in this disparate treatment? Do the benefits and protections of society not provide equal or greater value to the man of wealth as to the laborer?

Consistency: The inconsistencies and inequities of our current tax assessments are unconscionable, almost as though designed deliberately so that no two taxpayers will ever receive the same treatment. The greatest strength of my proposal is its underlying consistency. A constant and level assessment, even-handedly applied across the full spectrum of the populace, will minimize those inconsistencies and inequities and the corrupting manipulative favoritism that currently permeates our government and tax system.

A critical issue, of course, is ensuring that it is implemented as a single, constant assessment – *without reopening the door to political tinkering and favoritism.*

Caution and Restraint: Change never comes easily. Most of us prefer the *"Devil we know"* to the threat of the unknown. All challenges to the status quo are attacked as lacking caution and restraint. The classic defense of the status quo was succinctly summarized in the following quote by a British politician and writer referring to their parliamentary government.

"Defenders of the status quo will argue that this system has served us well over the centuries, that our parliamentary traditions have combined stability and flexibility and that we should not cast away in a minute what has taken generations to build."

— Ferdinand Mount (1939-)

Replace "parliamentary traditions" with "tax policies" in the preceding quote and you have the core argument that will undoubtedly be voiced against fundamental change of any sort. *"We should not cast away in a minute what has taken generations to build."* It has a good ring to it. It sounds like a compelling argument. But remember, what we have doesn't work – and I don't think tinkering with the current structure has a chance of changing that.

> I flatly reject the idea of imposing a VAT, or energy tax, or beverage tax, or any of the recently proposed add-on revenue fixes on top of the existing jury-rigged, dysfunctional mishmash we currently utilize. Every one of these regressive bolt-on options is guaranteed to make things worse instead of better, increasing burdens upon the portion of the population least able to carry them.
>
> Nor is it reasonable to think can we improve the situation by ratcheting up the "progressive" rate schedule or imposing a "millionaire's income tax surcharge". Experience has repeatedly reinforced the lesson that higher progressive rates applied to our current income tax structure are counter-productive because they discourage investment, retard growth and stimulate tax avoidance efforts. The wealthy will find a way to avoid them and they will fall crushingly upon the backs of the working middle class.

Any sense of existing "stability and flexibility" in the system we have is an illusion. On our present path we are either going to drown in a sea of debt and break the promises upon which our citizens are relying or we are going to break the back of the working middle class who are the drivers of our growth and productivity.

Furthermore, I believe reinforcing the principle of "equal application" to our tax code would fundamentally impose an element of caution that has been lost in our current structure. Is it cautious to proceed down a path that we all acknowledge is "unsustainable"? My concept and proposal, which combines what is essentially a flat tax proposal with a nominal asset tax, is designed to get us all back in the boat rowing together. It is designed to remove the illusion that governmental expenditures can be funded with Other People's Money. It is designed to defuse the class warfare that, on one hand calls out to "soak the rich", and on the other uses intellectually dishonest manipulations to pretend we have a progressive tax system while requiring a wage earner to pay higher tax rates than billionaire investors.

Key Issues:

Simplicity: An absolutely critical component of what I am advocating is its consistency and simplicity. I opened this chapter with a quote from H. L. Mencken which cautions against believing in simple solutions. I draw attention to it out of respect for caution and restraint. It is a caution I take seriously and a criticism I suspect will be leveled at these ideas. But, after consideration, I must respectfully disagree.

Mencken was an elitist with enormous disdain for the common man. He sneered at democracy and believed that society needed the leadership and guidance of "superior men". In this he had a lot in common with much of our current political class.

I believe there is far more hubris in thinking we are smart enough to tinker with and manage our economy than there is risk in relying upon simple core principles. I think you'll find the evidence is with me on this. One hardly needs to look farther than the recent real estate collapse and financial debacle. Our best and brightest assembled complex financial instruments, so complex they could only be understood by our best and brightest, and they anointed them the cure for all our ills. Their CLO's, CDO's, Credit Default Swaps and Derivative Instruments were so complex they couldn't really be explained, just *championed* – but since they came with the imprimatur of our "*best and brightest experts*", rated by independent agencies and insured by government sponsored entities, we relied upon them. Then they blew up.

> One of the common truisms of investing is, "If you can't understand it, don't trust it." People who trust in things they can't understand inevitably are at risk of investing with folks like Bernie Madoff.

After they blew up we transferred a very large part of the private losses into the public coffers – thereby teaching the architects of this debacle the important lesson that "they would be protected from their mistakes". If you're not angry about that you stand among a very small minority.

One of the reasons why our tax system has become so dysfunctional is that it's far too complex, so much so that we've lost sight of its simplest objective – to equitably allocate the cost of our government operations. It's not possible to write 2,500 page tax bills and have a balanced and foreseeable outcome. It's not possible to treat everybody differently and have a fair and equitable outcome.

Command and control, "managed" economies have an abysmal track record on almost all fronts: Growth, Efficiency, Innovation and Stability. So why are we heading down that path on so many different fronts?   When I recently listened to Larry Summers describe the panoply of tax breaks, credits, special incentives, and narrowly focused programs the administration is planning on unleashing in its efforts to jump-start the economy, I didn't know whether to scream or cry. That is hubris. It is delusional to believe that frantic, self-contradictory, unprincipled manipulation of the economy on multiple fronts can have foreseeable and balanced results. Those incentives certainly will have an impact. They will create winners and losers. But they won't lead us back to stability and prosperity.

I view simplicity and principle as virtues in government.

Investment Incentives: I anticipate the strongest arguments and objections against an asset tax will come from those among us who believe that taxing investment income is a disincentive to growth. There is a large body of work that supports that belief. I don't dispute it. I agree with it. Taxes on investment income do indeed act as a disincentive to productive investments. Today an enormous amount of effort goes into reducing "taxable income". As tax rates get higher, that effort accelerates. Our current tax code is complicit in the shell game.

But the people who use that argument to resist an asset tax may be missing the point. I'm proposing **repealing all taxes on investment income**. Today we manipulate investment decisions by playing with the tax code and thereby undermine the working of a free market economy. The cost of that manipulation, in addition to the purely financial cost, is a highly variable, sometimes capricious, distribution of the costs of government which I frankly find disturbingly inequitable.

An asset tax, as proposed, would remove those variable manipulative incentives, tax all accumulated wealth at a common nominal rate and *consistently reward the highest and best allocation of capital*, an objective I find highly desirable.

An Illustrative Example:

Four theoretical investors (let's call them Adam, Bob, Charlie and Dave) each have $1 million in accumulated investable capital. To keep things simple let's also assume they each have comparable jobs and expenses, with modest taxable earned incomes of $50,000 per year, which covers their expenses and puts them in the 25% federal tax bracket.

- Adam invests his $1 million in tax free bonds at 4.5%. He earns $45,000 per year from his investments. He pays zero tax on his investments.
- Bob invests actively and aggressively in the public markets. He makes a 10% annual return on his investments – all realized, all short term. He earns $100,000 which is taxed at his earned income rate. He pays $26,296 in tax on his investments. (His 25% tax rate jumps up to 28% for earnings above $106,800.)
- Charlie also invests in the public markets and has managed to earn the same 10% return as Bob. But unless it's offset by comparable losses, Charlie never sells anything in less than 366 days. So let's say half of Charlie's return is unrealized gains, and the other half, $50,000, is long-term capital gains. He pays the reduced long-term capital gains rate of 15%, or $7,500. So despite equaling Bob's investment return, Charlie pays 71.5% less tax.
- Dave took his $1 million, put 1/3 down, took out a $2 million mortgage, and bought a $3 million property in Montana. It has a lovely vacation house on it and a trout stream. It operates as a working farm, raising buffalo and breeding horses. Dave has a full time caretaker who runs the property very well. It manages to just break even every year. Included in its operating expenses are all the interest and loan costs, real estate taxes and maintenance, as well as the cost of Dave's four annual trips up to meet with his manager and review the results. During those trips, Dave usually brings along family and friends to whom he can brag about his investment. Of course, while they're there, Dave and his retinue usually spend six hours a day on the trout stream. Over the past decade or so real estate appreciation has averaged roughly 5%. So in rough numbers, Dave's $1 million equity investment has gained about $150,000 per year. But, of course, as long as he doesn't sell it, Dave pays no tax. When he does sell it he will pay a 15% long-term capital gain rate.

So, in my example, my four lucky millionaires[35] (yes, I won't argue, investment returns that reach 10% and 15% are indeed lucky outcomes) had investment gains that ranged from $45,000 to $150,000, reported taxable incomes that ranged from zero to $100,000, paid investment taxes that ranged from zero to $26,296 and

[35] Ladies, I apologize if my all male examples offend you. I tried mixing and matching genders but all I seemed to do was make things worse. When "Alice" invested in bonds my wife accused me of stereotyping a female risk profile. When "Danielle" created a tax shelter for her trout fishing expenses my wife stopped talking to me. Paired couples, i.e. "Bob and Betty", was just silly. So they're all male. Mea culpa.

combined to pay an aggregate tax total of $33,796, a mere 5.7% of their aggregate investment returns and roughly 0.8% of their invested capital.

Is there any part of that picture that doesn't look equitable to you?

Oh, wait. I forgot about Ernesto.

- Ernesto doesn't have any assets. He works with his hands and his back. He's a first generation immigrant, a proud naturalized citizen, and a very hard worker. He's ambitious and doing everything he can to give his children a better life and chance at the American Dream. He works 12 hours a day, six days a week. He's a skilled machinist and earns good money, almost $21.00/hour, $75,000 per year, thus 50% more than the earned incomes of Adam, Bob, Charlie and Dave. Since his extra $25,000 income comes in the form of wages, he and his employer each pays 7.65% in employment taxes in addition to his marginal federal tax rate of 25%. I'm going to credit him with his employer's portion and thus I calculate the total tax contribution resulting from his incremental $25,000 income is $10,075, or 40.3%. He pays more for his $25,000 incremental wages than Charlie does with a $100,000 investment return.

I could keep going, but presumably you're grasping the point. I'll do just one more.

- Fred has $200,000 of Earned Income in addition to his $1 million of invested assets. Last year Fred put his $1 million in a leveraged partnership managed by a successful hedge fund. At year end they reported his investment was worth $1,200,000, a 20% return on investment, consistent with their reported averages over the past 12 years. He's locked in for at least three years and can't take his money out, but it's structured so he has no income or current tax liability. Like Adam and Dave, Fred pays zero tax this year. When he does get his investment back it will be taxed at the 15% long-term capital gain rate. Treating Fred comparably with Ernesto (i.e. crediting him with the employer portion of SS/Med contributions) Fred's incremental tax liability is $53,111 on $150,000, or 35.4% versus Ernesto's 40.3%.

The Table on the following page summarizes key data from the preceding example and shows the disparate tax impact of current law, ranking them in order of the highest tax rate as a percent of Total Income and Appreciation. At 35.2% of Income, hard-working Ernesto pays the highest effective tax rate in the example.

Theoretical Tax Example
Existing Tax Burdens - 2009 Tax Tables
$Thousands

	Earned Income	Invstmt Income	Investment Returns		Total Taxes	Effective Rate (a)	
			Unrealized Gains	Total Income + Apprec		% of Income	% of Inc + Apprec
Ernesto	$75	$-		$75	$26.4	35.2%	35.2%
Bob	50	100		150	42.6	28.4%	28.4%
Fred	200		200	400	69.4	34.7%	17.4%
Adam	50	45		95	16.3	17.2%	17.2%
Charlie	50	50	50	150	23.8	23.8%	15.9%
Dave	$50		$150	$200	16.3	32.7%	8.2%

(a) Includes Employer portion of SS/MED

Fred, who earns 5.3 times as much as Ernesto, pays over twice as much tax, but at a rate slightly less than half as high. Dave, with 2.5 times the earnings, pays 38% less tax at an effective rate of only 8.2%.

It should be noted that the typical analysis of tax burdens omits all reference to SS/Med employment taxes, unrealized gains or other tax sheltered advantages provided by the law. But SS/Med contributions are real taxpayer burdens and unrealized gains represent real value. The only place where asset appreciation isn't income is on a tax return. At the end of the month or the year an investor doesn't evaluate how well he's done by looking at his taxable income – but by evaluating his asset balances and overall returns; thus, total earnings *inclusive of unrealized gains* is the proper benchmark to use. Yet even as a percent of taxable income, Ernesto pays the highest rate in this example and that is an *accurate depiction of the true relationship between all wage earners and investors.*

Once again I must repeat my question: Is there any part of this picture that doesn't look equitable to you?

If you can examine that chart and then explain to me with a straight face how our current tax system is more equitable and beneficial than what I'm proposing, I want to hear from you.

WHAT WOULD MY PROPOSAL CHANGE?

My 2% Solution would require each lucky millionaire to pay 2% of his accumulated wealth in taxes, subject to a minimum threshold exclusion (for illustrative purposes I will assume $250,000). A common rate, a common exclusion = *Equal Treatment.* Yes, it would result in a tax increase. Yes, we Americans have acquired a reflex reaction that rejects any and all proposed tax increases. But we can't keep our heads in the sand forever and what I'm looking for is an equitable way to reform our tax system and balance the budget.

In the example previously outlined, my five theoretical investors had aggregate investment returns of $595,000 but only $195,000 of that was income and only $150,000 was taxable. This is not a scientific sample by any means, but it is representative of the range of alternatives. Under current law and practice three of those hypothetical investors paid zero investment tax, one paid over $26,000 and the total investment tax assessed was less than $34,000.

Assuming a $250,000 exclusion and adjusting period ending asset balances to reflect the varying investment returns, I've projected asset tax assessments for the members of my example to range from $15,000 to $19,000 for an aggregate of $103,000[36]. If you compare that to the $34,000 current tax bill your heart might

---

36 *For reference Appendix IV* provides a detailed schedule of the assumptions and results of this theoretical example and analysis.

jump into your throat because you will see a 200% tax increase. But $103,000 is only 17.3% of the $595,000 return on assets – representing half the tax rate currently assessed to most wages and salaries. It is a barely noticeable increase over the current long-term capital gain rate of 15% and a discount to short term capital gains taxes, both of which it replaces. It is also offset by elimination of the corporate income tax and estate and inheritance taxes. Yes, it does tax gains on an annual basis. Yes, it does eliminate the tax benefit of writing off investment losses. And yes, it would in some instances significantly redistribute the overall tax burden, since it would link it to wealth, not realized net profits. But if one sets aside self-interest in using the tax code for personal advantage, those are all virtues, not flaws. Investment risks and rewards are placed back on the investor – not shared or underwritten by the IRS.

If you can explain how my proposed 2% Net Asset Tax would distort investment decisions and activity more than our current hodgepodge of deduction and credits, I want to hear from you.

Tying up assets in risk free municipal bonds or illiquid investments would become less attractive. But investors will be *more strongly incented to seek productive investment opportunities* because existing tax benefits for non-productive or low risk investments will be removed. An asset tax will not be an incentive to investors to shy away from risk and stuff their cash under the mattress or leave their assets parked in unproductive investments just so they don't have to pay the tax. Elimination of the disincentives to reallocating investments should make the capital markets more liquid and productive, not less so.

How would it work?

Just as surely as some people will challenge my theory as too simplistic, others will claim it is far too complex to implement, and trot out a variety of complaints about the impact it will have, particularly on illiquid assets. So, although it seems a bit premature to advance discussion beyond the conceptual overview already set forth, I will expand very, very briefly on how I think it might be implemented.

Addressing the Two Tiered Income Tax, let me first acknowledge that I can't really tell whether the proper Second Tier Maximum rate should be 25% or 30%, but I believe that that is the range. The objective is a revenue neutral flattening of the earned income tax schedules which eliminates both the fiction of separate employment taxes and the rat's nest of exceptions, exclusions, deductions and credits that Washington uses to bribe constituents and reward campaign contributors. As described in Chapter 4, the nearly impenetrable Machiavellian manipulation of the tax code makes it impossible for an outsider to accurately evaluate the impact of any change. That manipulation is one of the reasons why actual tax revenues lag so far behind rates in published tax schedules. Despite tax rates that start at 10% and rise to 35%, net collections from taxable returns in 2007 were only 13.8%. As a narrower example, in 2007, actual tax collections on incomes (reported adjusted gross income) between $50,000 and $100,000 were 9%, despite published rate schedules that place them at or above 30%. Unfortunately, the impact of lower investment tax rates can't be extracted with information I obtained from OMB publications. That said, I'll stand by my guesstimate that a rate somewhere between 25% and 30% should be revenue neutral. Today the nominal minimum tax rate is 10%, but, as repeatedly cited, after all the adjustments and gyrations Congress and the IRS apply, the aggregate net rate applied to all taxable incomes is *only 3.8% higher.* While a more conservative guess of a revenue neutral rate might be 27.5%, my personal judgment leans toward the lower range, but *only if all the exclusions and deductions are stripped away.* (Except for dependent exemptions.)

The base tax rate of 15% should start with the first dollar of income, as do the current SS/Med taxes which would be eliminated.   (Employee reported gross payrolls would get a 7.65% bump, the fiction of "Employer Contributions" would be eliminated and net take-home pay would remain stable.)   Current (2009) tax schedules bump the federal tax rate to 25% at $33,950 which is as sound a threshold for the bump as I have a basis to suggest. For simplicity, in modeling sample data I have used a $35,000 threshold.

Deductions and exclusions and further manipulative tinkering with the taxable base should be strictly eliminated. The Second Tier step-up, whether it rise to a maximum of 25%, 27.5% or 30%, should be designed to make the replacement of earned income and SS/MED taxes revenue neutral.

> ***The nominal rates for all taxpayers will decline.*** Taxpayers with incomes under $34,000 will see their nominal rate decline from 25.3% or 30.3%, to 15%. The existing maximum 40.3% rate (applicable to income between $33,950 and $106,800) will drop by at least 10.3 percentage points (a full 15.3% points if the maximum rate can be held to only 25%).
>
> The revenue lost thru these nominal reductions will be replaced by eliminating the multitude of special incentives and deductions, predominately aimed at the wealthier portion of the citizenry, which today create flagrantly unequal treatment under the tax code.

Moving on to the asset assessments, despite the howls, protests and objections I anticipate arising against this concept, it is hard for me to imagine that an asset tax could be more unwieldy, inequitable, or susceptible to manipulation than income and profit taxes. It is, however, helpful to break it down into its various components and think through the variations.

I perceive three major categories of assets:

- Liquid Assets/Investments,
- Illiquid Assets/Investments, and
- Personal Property.

In broad terms, Liquid Assets are items which are both readily marketable and easy to value and Illiquid Assets are infrequently traded and, thus, more uncertain and challenging to accurately value. I am using the term Personal Property rather loosely (and more narrowly than many accounting or legal definitions might) to describe purchased items which depreciate through personal use. As an example: excepting classic collectibles, most personal automobiles, while they have tangible value, do not hold value or appreciate over time. An even more obvious example would be clothing. Unless the item in question once belonged to Marilyn Monroe or Elvis, it is not going to be confused with an investment asset. If the item in question did belong to Marilyn Monroe or Elvis, it's now become an investment asset so it no longer qualifies as personal property.

While there may be additional subcategories and some overlap between them, if you think of assets in these broad terms first it's fairly easy to conceptualize their treatment.

Liquid Assets, primarily cash and marketable securities, are easy. You establish their value as of a specified date, calculate the tax liability and pay it. As a general rule, Liquid Assets are not only readily marketable, they are marketable in fractions; so if you have to liquidate a portion of your holdings it is not a significant obstacle. I would propose assessments be made as of 12/31 of the tax year and payments be due in quarterly installments over the following year. All assessments, including marketable securities, should be based on the fair market value net of related debt. So if securities have been bought on margin the tax is assessed against the holder's equity value. (The loan will be taxed on the other side of the transaction as an asset of the issuer.)

Personal Property (per my narrow definition) is also easy. It should be excluded from taxable assets.

I will leave it to somebody else to develop detailed rules and regulations of when an item is or is not personal property; and there will be rules required. Because while I'm comfortable categorizing your three year old Ford Fiesta as personal property and saying it ought to be excluded from the tax base, I don't want to encourage anyone to pay cash for a Lamborghini so they can claim it's not a taxable asset. So maybe it is not as easy as it looks. A rowboat or ski boat may be personal property. A world cup racing yacht probably is not.

Nevertheless, the conceptual issue isn't very complicated and, if my proposal manages to gain traction, it may create a surplus of tax accountants, some of whom can turn their attention to whatever rules and regulations are required. One alternative might be to tax personal property, but make it subject to a separate exclusion, say $100,000 which should easily shelter the value of two family cars and a small household of furniture, but would capture the value of a fleet of Ferraris or a warehouse of Louis XIV antiques. A second alternative would be to simply incorporate a reasonable personal property allowance in the overall exclusion. My point is not to resolve the issue but simply to acknowledge it and show that it is not truly a substantive obstacle.

Illiquid Assets, of course, raise complications which require still more thought and, perhaps, some additional flexibility.

Illiquid assets include a number of subcategories:

- Real Estate
- Privately held Corporations and Businesses
- Partnerships, Trusts and LLC's
- Antiques, Art & Collectibles

By definition, unique and infrequently traded assets are harder (and typically more subjective) to value, and often cannot be liquidated in fractions. People will claim that the liquidity and valuation challenges of such assets are subject to such extreme complication as to make the entire proposal unworkable. However, the falsity of that claim becomes readily apparent when you take the time to think it through.

Real Estate comprises the most obvious and familiar category of illiquid asset, and claiming that it cannot be fairly and accurately assessed and valued is simply silly. We do it all the time today. Properties of all types are regularly appraised today for the purposes of both loan applications and tax rolls. Could we value them more consistently and accurately? Probably. Should we? Certainly. But claiming we can't do it is simply silly. We can and should establish sound, consistent Fair Market Appraisal policies and practices to use as the basis for tax assessments, requiring licensed appraisals at least every three to five years (and precluding using an inflated appraisal for loan applications and a conflicting depressed appraisal for tax purposes). But valuation uncertainties are not a legitimate obstacle.

Objections about the liquidity burden annual taxation would place upon property owners have some validity, but at least in my opinion, prompt one of two responses; either a shrug of indifference, or a reasonable payment finance/deferral option.

It is possible that there could be individuals with land-wealth which exceeds a minimum tax threshold, but who do not possess liquid assets from which to pay their tax burden. Today, like Dave from my earlier example, people can avoid taxes by parking their wealth in real estate which generates no income. I am proposing that option should be eliminated. As a matter of principle, if one recognizes that the protection of wealth is one of the greatest benefits our government provides, it readily follows that the holders of wealth should be assessed their fair contribution to those costs of government. If you can't otherwise afford to pay your contribution toward maintaining our government and society you can't afford to own the property.

That said, I also would be a strong advocate of providing financing for deferred payment of 50% of the tax liability on illiquid assets. Holders of real estate or other illiquid assets should be able to pay 1% in cash, and finance the balance by paying interest-only quarterly at a modest statutory rate – say 2.5% above the ten year Treasury note. Balances deferred on such a basis would retain a senior secured priority claim against the property, be limited to no more than 50% of appraised value and payable upon sale or transfer of the property.

Privately Held Corporations and Businesses are a little more complicated, but not outrageously so. Assessing taxes based upon acquisition costs and accumulating book value for the first three years and requiring business valuations every three years thereafter to keep pace with fair market changes would conceptually be viable. Business valuations may be more subjective than real estate, but they are used today for trust, inheritance and estate tax assessments, divorce settlements and many other purposes. Certainly there might be temptation for owners to attempt to understate values. But a combination of licensed appraisers, IRS valuation audits, and strict penalties on cheating (e.g., steep fines for infractions or perhaps even mildly confiscatory recapture taxes on sales effected at prices more than 20% higher than tax reported valuations?) should provide a reasonable basis for assessing asset tax liabilities. There's little reason to think that tax avoidance strategies aimed at minimizing a 2% asset assessment would be nearly as aggressively followed or inventively pursued as those now used to avoid profit taxes.

Partnerships, Trusts and LLCs conceptually are even simpler than privately held businesses in that partners and shareholders currently receive at least annual valuation statements and the managers of those entities are typically incented upon the reported annual performance and valuation gains. Thus, in theory, manager-generated statements of year end value should provide simple and viable tax base statements. However, regulatory oversight and caution will undoubtedly have to be applied to these entities, or else they could develop into a new hotbed of tax avoidance inventiveness. But here again, the incentive to avoid a 2% asset tax remains less than current incentives to suppress or shield profits.

My final category of illiquid assets, *Antiques, Art and Collectibles*, has its own unique characteristics which confuse the issue a bit more, but since the category size is substantially smaller than all the others, definitive treatment is less critical. In principle, Fair Market Value should remain the target criteria, however, taxing these assets at the higher of acquisition cost or insured value would probably serve as an effective proxy without the complication and expense of requiring periodic reappraisals. Perhaps requiring periodic appraisals of individual assets exceeding $500,000 or $1 million (covering Grand Master paintings and the like) would be appropriate.

So there it is, in roughly six pages an outline of how to structure and implement a 2% asset tax through which to a) broaden the tax base and b) seek a fairer contribution toward the costs of government from the wealthy and privileged while c) simultaneously eliminating the manipulative and counter-productive disincentives which exist in today's investment tax policies.

What have I missed?

NON-PROFITS

One of the first warnings I heard when I started floating these concepts and ideas in a small circle of associates was that it would trigger a massive flow of assets into trusts and non-profits. This of course raises the question of whether or why trusts and non-profits should be assessed the asset tax?

I believe the answer is obvious. They should.

Clearly generation-skipping trusts and other, as yet un-imagined, structures designed specifically to continue shielding wealth from taxation must not be perpetuated. The objective is to make the entire wealth of society subject to a modest assessment in contribution to the costs of government. But even more broadly, I would propose that all non-profits be subject to the asset tax.

Frankly, irrespectively of whether the asset tax is applied to most non-profits, I fully anticipate that some of the loudest voices against the proposal I am putting forth will arise from the non-profit community which currently relies not only upon tax immunity for their operations, but more importantly tax avoidance among their benefactors as incentive for contributions. I've always felt that buying "charity" through tax deductions was simply another way the privileged get the government to provide preference for their pet projects and government hides some of its poor disbursement choices.

I've always loved the theatre. That doesn't mean government should fund it – not even one of every three dollars via a tax deduction. There are people who think that symphony orchestras, classical and modern dance, and opera will not survive without tax-sheltered contributions. I think they're wrong. But if they're not wrong, so be it. Whether it be an Arts, Education or Religious institution, any non-profit that needs 35% marginal tax rates and tax deductibility of contributions to justify donations should rethink its mission and its operating budget.

Currently the government uses tax deductible incentives to funnel money to projects they often couldn't justify if they had to fund them with a direct vote. I think we should stop that. Even if it is only one of every three dollars, letting a third party reach into the government coffers to redirect tax dollars to support private choices and bypass the budgetary decision process is inappropriate.

Other People's Money is an insidious and persistent evil. It typically sounds innocuous, but in practice it is surprising how universally it results in unsound unintended consequences.

Despite the best intentions, the cost of a college education has sky-rocketed. Universities accumulate multi-billion dollar endowments and build stunning edifices, but tuition outpaces inflation every year. Universities pay generous fees to investment managers. They can pay a 2% asset tax.

Some religious entities have amassed vast fortunes. Like Universities, they pay generous fees to investment managers. They also can pay a 2% asset tax.

It is of course not very difficult to imagine scenarios that seem to deserve treatment as exception. But exceptions should be avoided.

Charity toward worthy causes will always be present in the American individual. Many of the most truly charitable causes receive their greatest support from the lower and middle classes – the $5.00 and $10.00 donations to Haiti, Feed the Children, UNICEF, the local community theatre. If we flatten rates and provide tax relief to the working middle class, those charitable impulses will not be suppressed. We may actually make charitable giving easier and more affordable. Worthy causes will always find support in America. Worthy charities should not require bribery through the tax code.

Projects that deserve government support can continue to receive it, but they should be funded through a normal appropriations process, subject to vote, through which government applies *equal treatment* in assessing taxes and responsibly dispenses *our money*.

What other objections might I have missed?

I will be looking to you, the readers, to fill my gaps and identify any errors and omissions.

AN IMPORTANT FINAL NOTE RE:
POTENTIAL OBJECTIONS

Another objection I anticipate will be raised against this proposal is that **we *simply can't trust the government with our money*.** Unfortunately, it is an objection that has a factual justification.

One of the core objectives and justifications for the proposal I have formulated is balancing the budget. As explained at length in Chapter 5, if the incremental tax revenues are used to balance the budget there should be a very advantageous trade-off between an annual 2% asset tax and stability of the currency.

But while constricting government revenues has proven to be a totally ineffective means of imposing discipline over expenditures, there is a risk that increasing revenues may stimulate even higher spending.

The only potential unintended consequence I can imagine that would have greater risk than the path we are on now is if Congress were to implement a plan of this sort, massively raising taxes, and then proceed to continue running trillion dollar deficits.

This is one of the reasons I believe we cannot simply change tax policy – we must change the fundamental political environment and return to responsible Citizen Representatives.

The difficult decisions required to control runaway government program costs can only come when our law-making representatives think and act on behalf of the broad public interest (not narrow fractions of their constituents) and if they manage the budget as though they are spending their own money. Yes, I believe the wealthy are not presently paying their fair share and, yes, I am proposing changes that will redistribute the tax burden so that it applies to wealth as well as income. But I am not advocating a "Tax the Rich" reform. I am advocating a fundamental change in tax structure and process in order to eliminate existing gross and capricious disparities in tax treatment. I am advocating a principled move toward equal treatment and away from the practice of pitting different classes of citizens one against the other. Tax law must strive for principled equal treatment. Tax law should be no different than criminal law – the willful design of special treatment for separate classes of citizen's must be eliminated.

"Tax the Rich" reforms, which say we will only raise taxes on a small segment of the population, move in exactly the opposite direction – toward *unequal treatment*... and they exacerbate our problems. Today our lawmakers think that when they fund projects and policies with Other People's Money, or deficits, those projects are free. They are not.

Counter-intuitive though it may seem the "Pay-Go" tax reform process, which Congress pretends to be a tool to control new spending, has actually made the situation worse. It has reinforced their tendency to segment the population and pay for one faction's benefits with another faction's money. The process of paying for targeted programs with targeted tax revenues needs to stop. Every time a government expenditure or policy is authorized we need to recognize that a piece of it comes out of everyone's pocket. My 2% Solution is a proposal for stable and consistent tax rates applied to both earned income and *accumulated wealth*. It is designed to re-impose that critical requirement of equal treatment and the sense of individual responsibility and burden that comes with it.

PART VI

A CALL TO ARMS

"Never doubt that a small group of thoughtful, committed citizens can change the world. Indeed, it is the only thing that ever has."
— Margaret Mead (1901–1978)

CHAPTER 13

BECOME AN
AGENT OF CHANGE

What now?

First, for those of you who made it this far, thank you for your time and interest. I recognize that I may very well be shouting impotently into the teeth of a raging storm. But at least I've made an attempt. Even if you disagree and reject my ideas, I appreciate you joining me in that attempt.

I am not a big-money political contributor. I'm not in a position to be. Nor, as you may by now know, would I choose to be even if I had the resources to do so. I disapprove of buying and selling political access and influence.

But I am a believer in this Democratic Republic of ours and this has been my attempt to be a participant in the process of government and the conversation about what kind of society and government we are going to hand over to our children. I am a believer in the influence of ideas. This book is my attempt to put that belief into practice.

Until I started this process I did not understand the extent of our founders' concern and caution about the Democratic process. It has become apparent to me now that they clearly understood the risks of the popular vote and the potential tyranny of the majority, and they foresaw the need for vigilance in the execution and evolution of government. In some respects I doubt they would have been as surprised as I have been by many of the twists toward self-dealing and protection of the status quo that have developed over the years in our Congress. I also doubt they would have stood still for them.

Once again, I believe that fundamental change is imperative.

If I'm wrong, it doesn't matter. If I'm just an outlying crank, tilting at windmills, spotting ghosts in the shadows where there are none, then no action is needed. I will have wasted quite a lot of my time and a little bit of yours. But in that case this book won't reach a very wide audience and will thus hardly be noticed.

However, if you have come this far without abandoning me, perhaps it is because you share at least some of my concerns?

Where to Start?

> *"We have met the enemy and he is us."*
> — Pogo - by Walt Kelly (1913-1973)

Start by recognizing that we are the problem. Just as we are the people, we are the government… and we are the problem. It's not them versus us – it's us.

Before anything else is possible, the public has to change its expectations and make its new requirements known.

My goal with this book has been to initiate a dialogue and discussion. My modest intent of merely adding to the policy options has changed. I initially set out to perform and provide some factual analysis, examine alternative perspectives and urge more open discussion of the tax policy challenges which are widely known, but just as widely ignored. However, it's become clear to me that merely prodding the establishment to shift its view and examine new tax policy options would be to ignore the more pressing problems I think we face.   It also would fail to work. Because unless something shakes our Congress up and forces them to look past the next election cycle to the larger responsibilities they hold, current incentives and existing allegiances will conspire to leave them with their heads in the sand, protecting the status quo and pretending they are doing the public's bidding.

Once again, if I'm wrong, it doesn't matter.   But ask yourself the following questions:

- Do you believe that our American Democracy is moving forward in a positive direction and needs no better guidance?
- Do you believe our money-filled electoral process is providing us with the government we deserve?
- Do you believe our tax policies are sound, productive and fair?
- Do you believe our elected officials already are acting as Citizen Representatives, with incentives fully aligned with the rest of the population?

If, after consideration, your answer to each of those questions is a confident "Yes", then I'm frankly surprised you made it all the way through the book. So, again, I enthusiastically thank you for your interest and participation. You've invested a couple of hours giving a fair hearing to my observations, opinions, concerns and suggestions about the budget and political process. I can't ask for more.

But what if you join me in believing that the answer to each of these questions is "No"? If you find truth in what I have said in this book and share some of the concerns I set forth, *what then?* If that's the case, then I must respectfully suggest that there is more for you to do.

The next step is to explore these questions in greater detail yourself. Share them with others. Make these ideas (better yet, your ideas and reactions developed in response to the ideas I've set out) a matter for further exploration and discussion.

Think about the questions, the perspectives, the challenges and suggestions I've made. Test them in your own mind. If you find something of value, share it with friends. Let them question it. Then broaden the circle of discussion. Utilize any access you might have to larger circles of influence. Write to the editor of your favorite publication. Push your questions upon the media. Make your questions and concerns become part of a wide-ranging dialogue and discussion.

If I am not alone in believing that bringing home the bacon for narrow constituencies is an inappropriate directive for our representatives, then we need to make our view known. We need to change our expectations and directions. We need to stop and think about the core values of the American Character. If freedom, liberty, and self-reliance, each combined with a sense of community, are indeed core American values then we should stop instructing our politicians to act like greedy bickering factions. If we believe in equal opportunity, and have faith that seeking a path to mutual benefit is both ethically right and the most effective means to achieve a flourishing society we should stop allowing Congress to support either Crony Capitalism or a Nanny State reliance upon government. Crony Capitalism is both ethically wrong and damaging to the goal of equal opportunity. And no matter how well-intentioned, Command and Control Government policies imposed by a Nanny State are both ineffective and an infringement of the liberty upon which our Republic is based.

We do get the government we deserve. We cannot expect our government to be better than we are. If we have been veering toward the wrong path, then collectively and individually, we must provide our influence and guidance to re-shape the direction of our future.

We can't count on someone else to do it. It must be a joint, collective and substantial effort. I can, and will, try to stimulate a conversation. I will send copies of this book to my Congressmen. I will try to get copies into the hands of political commentators and media representatives. But if it's just my voice, it won't be heard. They probably won't even read it.

If I were just advocating a minor change in tax policy, there is a very small chance it could gain traction based on ideas alone. But not this suggestion. This is a call for fundamental changes in the structure and approach to representative government. It is a wake-up call to our representatives, a reminder that they were called to public service to provide their judgment on our collective behalf, not to serve as protectors of the interests of their campaign contributors. It is a reminder that they must not serve narrowly, focused on the next election cycle, but broadly, focused on the stability and prosperity of the Union.

This message of challenge to the status quo will only be heard if it is delivered by many insistent voices.

> Presumably, it's already become obvious, but if not, I'll be a bit more express. One of the key influences that made me undertake to write this treatise was my observation that over the past year, Congress has embarked on the greatest expansion in the scope of government that has been attempted in at least 50 years.
>
> It was not my intention to participate directly in the debate about the merits or dangers of that particular expansion so much as to voice my concern that the existing perspective and incentives of our policy makers – specifically their professional self-interest and allegiances to narrow constituencies, if left unchecked, will irrevocably take us down the wrong path. No matter how they dress it up with "good intentions", so long as dishonest discourse remains the norm and narrow self-interest the driver, we cannot expect our leaders to guide us to confront the difficult and complicated decisions required to maintain the balanced goals of our society. Furthermore, now that they've succeeded in that expansion, we are going to have to find a way to pay for it.
>
> There is no free lunch. We cannot spend our way to prosperity with other people's money.
>
> At the outset, I pointed out that I have long been a fiscal conservative (approaching libertarian). But that, and the fact that much of what I've cited has been in reference to actions taken by the current administration, shouldn't be construed as indicating much support for the Republicans. Though in the past, and in their stated platforms, I have often found more to like from moderate Republicans than from the "nanny" voice of

the Democrat's, the Republicans' grotesque failure to implement any fiscal restraint in practice and the manner in which they have embraced the harsh, extreme and intolerant voices of the Republican religious right, have left them morally bankrupt observers in this travesty we call government.

I have considered the rise of the Tea Party element over the last few months a very mixed signal. On the one hand, it has been encouraging to see that grass roots activism remains alive and kicking in the Republic. On the other, it is distressing to me how much of the energy seems to be misdirected. Most specifically, to the extent the Tea Party mantra remains the discredited idea that we can reduce taxes and somehow starve government in order to make them cut expenditures, they are not only wrong, they are being irresponsible.

Tax increases are not only inevitable, they are necessary. Voting out an irresponsible incumbent simply to reestablish his equally irresponsible opponent would not represent progress. We need tax reform and responsibility in government, not more of the same failed policies and political pandering.

If we, the electorate, choose to send a message to Congress we must be careful not to let them learn the wrong lessons.

So back to practicalities. What is it I want? What is it I am urging upon you?

First, I want your opinions and your insights. I want you to help me test my theory. I want you to help me find the flaws in my logic. I truly do want you to tell me if and where I've gone wrong. And if I have gone wrong, perhaps I will still have stimulated someone else to find a better path.

You can do that in two ways.

1. You can share your opinions directly, and
2. You can join me in demanding these questions be addressed by a broader selection of experts, urging them to do so, to the greatest extent possible, with an open mind.

I've established a website at www.2PctSolution.com through which I will attempt to accumulate direct opinions and responses to my proposed ideas. I intend to set up a survey that I will maintain and monitor, and I intend to post the results and reactions as accumulated. Please participate in providing your responses and reactions. I do ask you not to try to stuff the ballot box. Obviously I will not be able to claim the results as a scientific sampling of reactions or opinions, but I will be making efforts to screen out multiple submissions and am seeking to accumulate unique reactions.

With regard to obtaining a more expert review and analysis, if you find merit in what I've set forth I'd like you to add your voice to mine. There are many ways in which you can do that. My personal first choice would be to see a million copies of my book physically delivered to Congress by a million separate citizens. That would grab some attention. (It would have the added benefit of increasing book sales – which wouldn't hurt my ego either.) But, kidding aside, while it would be effective, it isn't really necessary to physically deliver multiple copies of books that probably wouldn't be read. *It is necessary to raise your voice and be heard.* What might a handful of voices accomplish? The quote from Margaret Mead that opens this chapter says it all. Every new idea has to start somewhere… from someone. A few thoughtful voices really can make a difference.

So pick up a pen. Pick up a telephone. Fire off an email. Add your name to a petition.

If I've convinced you and you share my reasoning and rationale, tell your neighbor and your Congressman about it. Pass this book on for someone else to read. If I've merely intrigued you, tell them that. I'll make it easy for you. On pages 203 and 204 I've drafted two alternative statements, one expressing Support and one expressing Intrigue. If your opinion aligns with either one of them, tear it out, sign your name to it and send it off to your Congressman or favorite media editor. Make copies and send it to everyone you know.

I've also posted them as Petitions at www.2PctSolution.com. Log on and add your name; I'll compile a tally. (Again, please don't stuff the ballot box; it will be more meaningful if every name is unique.) Download the pdf file and forward it to everyone you think might be interested. Send it to people you think should be, even if they're not.

If one of these statements doesn't fit your view – draft your own. Mark it up and change it. Start from scratch and express yourself in your own words. Help me force a dialogue on the issue.

Don't trust me. I've been talking to myself. Maybe I've talked myself down a blind alley? That's why I want to demand a broader dialogue and review. Send it to your favorite Sunday morning talking head or favorite news periodical and ask for their response. But don't trust them as "experts" either. Remember, that's how we got the financial melt-down. Make them address and disprove challenges to the status quo, not just dismiss them. Make them explain why what we are doing today works. Make them explain how the Social Security trust fund is anything other than a fraud. Make them explain why no one cares that the working class pays a higher tax burden than big money political donors. Make them explain why a regressive European VAT makes more sense than a modest asset tax. Make them debate and explain what merit they see in expanding regressive consumption taxes vs. implementing a 2% asset tax.

By the way - If you reject everything I've said – tell them that, too. And tell me. Tell me why. Tell me where I've gone wrong. Provide me, your neighbors, and your Congressmen with a *better answer*… if you have one. We need one.

So much for tax policy. Now what about the political process?

I urge you to join me in taking an activist role in demanding more from our political process. We have to start by demanding honesty.

When our politicians step forward and say "I did not have sex with that woman", or "I did not father that child", we can shake our heads in disgust, feel sympathy for their spouses, and choose to forgive their human weaknesses. Or not.

But when the administration claims that they are guaranteeing 30 million people health care without increasing costs or taking a dime from anyone making less than $250,000 per year… we have to call them out as liars[37]. When Republicans accuse Democrats of trying to "ration" health care – pandering to the public's worst fears and emotions – instead of seizing the opportunity to engage in meaningful conversation and debate about the fact we desperately need to "rationalize" health care… we need to call them out as duplicitous cowards.

When politicians of either stripe act like opportunistic con men… we have to vote them out of office. We all know when they lie to us. We are complicit in allowing them to do it.

We need to make some fundamental changes in our expectations and processes. It will not be a rapid change because every time we vote someone out we have to vote someone in – and the candidates on both sides of the ballot all have the same character flaw. We require it of them.

So once again, step one in implementing any fundamental change in how our politicians operate will be to communicate a change in our requirements. If we, as Citizens, can't set aside our individual short-term self-interests and change our perspectives we can't expect our politicians to do it of their own volition.

Specifically, what do I think we need to do?

- Demand Honest Discourse
- Laud and Encourage Political Character and Principle
- Demand Exercise of Judgment
- Disavow "Bringing Home the Bacon"

---

[37] Despite all other merits the policy might have, it is baldly dishonest semantics to claim that forcing individuals to buy coverage is different from imposing a tax.

- Vote the Bums Out
- Demand Campaign Finance Reform

I do think it's possible to change the attitude and approach in Washington. In some areas it's already started. I am encouraged by the citizen's of Nebraska and Nevada who have stepped forward to express their disgust with Ben Nelson and Harry Reid's public bribery deal enacted as part of the Senate Health Care bill. It is encouraging to see the citizen's of Nebraska step up and say, "We don't want to be part of that. We don't believe that's how government should operate," even though it was aimed at putting money back in their pockets.

I hope the citizens of Nebraska and Nevada follow through and vote Nelson and Reid both out of office. It would serve as a shot across the bow of every member of Congress.

I wish the citizen's of Ohio would exhibit similar resolve and throw John Boehner out on his ear. I strongly urge his constituents to vote him out: for his irresponsible, gleeful charge that passage of the health care bill would trigger Armageddon; for his role in the Republicans' irresponsible refusal to engage in meaningful debate on the health care issue; and for his irresponsible leadership with regard to tax policy. While his well-publicized refusal to participate in taking earmarks is highly commendable, his leadership on these other issues has been disgraceful. Sending him packing would be a patriotic act because the Republicans need a shot across their bow as well – to keep them from learning the wrong lesson.

Frankly, if I had my way, every incumbent on both sides of the aisle who was up for reelection in 2010 and 2012 would be turned out of office. Bar none. A message for all. Business as usual is over. If the 90/10 incumbent reelection advantage were suddenly reversed, our political class would be forced to take notice.

Might that be a bit harsh? Perhaps. Might that be unfair? Absolutely. As I've said before, they are what we've made them. They are what we've required them to be: self-interested chameleons. But we can't afford to let it continue and the change has got to start somewhere.

Do I believe such a harsh response would be dangerous? Not particularly. Our governmental structure is resilient. It's hard for me to imagine that shuffling the chairs at random for an election cycle or two would do more damage than our elected officials are doing left to their own devices. As I said before, I'd rather pick representatives the same way we pick jurors than see candidates continue to buy their way into office with political contributions.

My real concern is that if we, the voting public, exercise our displeasure with only the power of our votes, we still won't get fresh blood into office because our system populates the ticket from both parties with cogs from broken machines. The winners (by default) would in all likelihood misinterpret the message.

The problem with expressing displeasure primarily against the party in power is that the minority party will hear what they want to hear, a vote of confidence for their policy positions, rather than what they need to hear, a warning and rebuke against the broken process.

So instead of relying and focusing strictly upon the vote in the next election cycle, I believe we should focus upon the message.   Unless we are ready to change the message,… Unless we are ready to change the requirements we place upon our elected officials,… I don't think we stand a very good chance of achieving the kind of fundamental shift in governing philosophy that I am advocating.

Are we ready to disavow "bringing home the bacon"? Apparently many of our fellow citizens from Nebraska are. God Bless them for that. How about the rest of us? Are we ready to demand an honest discussion about health care? Are we willing to pay for the benefits we demand? Are we willing to forego the benefits we are not prepared to pay for? Or are we going to continue to demand our Representatives lie to us? Are we going to continue demanding more benefits and more services accompanied by lower taxes?

> *Health Care Redux* – The recently enacted Health Care Law is highly illustrative of the dysfunctional and dangerous state of the current governmental process. The Democrats are celebrating a substantial victory in the fact that they managed to pass "something", irrespective of the fact that they attacked a small problem (lack of universal coverage) while exacerbating a large one (uncontrolled costs). Not a week had passed following passage before President Obama acknowledged in an interview on NBC's Today Show that "this was just the first step". Time after time, advocates of the governmental expansion acknowledged that what they were passing didn't tackle the real problem – but they considered the principle of universal healthcare access so important they viewed passage of the entitlement as more important than the workability or cost of the programs being enacted. Repeatedly the bill's advocates acknowledged that, as written, the bill was problematic, but it was more important to do *something* than to do the right thing.
>
> The Republicans acted even less responsibly. They fought to "kill the bill" as a political strategy. Acting as political opportunists, the Republican leadership aborted any meaningful dialogue about "What minimum level of services ought to be provided to our citizens?" and "At what cost?" Instead, they characterized

all conversation about cost containment considerations as the first step toward Killing Granny. Worse yet, this despicable and cowardly approach to the important challenges of government cannot be blamed upon the lunatic fringe; it was championed by the party leaders.

As a result, what did we get? An undefined, unlimited, and unfunded new entitlement.

Now, promptly following the bill's passage, Attorneys General from nearly two dozen states are poised to continue the fight against the bill in the courts – seeking to overturn it on technical grounds as an unconstitutional expansion of Federal Powers and infringement of States' Rights. Of course, they're right. The bill is a massive expansion of government built upon lies and Other People's Money – pretending that mandates upon the young and healthy aren't taxes and continuing to downstream irresponsible cost burdens to state governments. But, in typical fashion, they are focused on the wrong issue. The constitutionality of the health care entitlement should not be fought as a technicality. It is central to the issue.

Health care reform of this nature and magnitude should never have been addressed in a 2,700 page legislative monstrosity. Insurance reform could have and should have been addressed in a more modest and discreet legislative package. But universal entitlement to medical care should have been addressed as a constitutional amendment. The scope and limits of entitlements deserve to receive honest debate; but instead of crafting and defining a guiding principle, Congress horse-traded its way to an incomprehensible manipulative hodgepodge of special deals and incentives.

In 2009 we watched government at its worst: good intentions and hubris, combined with lies and OPM, resulting in legislation that appears poised to make a bad situation worse.

Don't misunderstand, I am not an advocate of trying to repeal the law. But I am pointing out that we've made things much, much harder for ourselves by doing it the wrong way. Because the task of defining how much we can and should do, and how much we are willing to pay for it, still remains ahead of us. Only now we have to debate how much we are going to take away from people, rather than how much we can provide. How are we going to do that? Certainly, our political leaders haven't displayed a willingness or ability to guide those difficult choices in anything they've done to date.

How can we possibly change that?

I see only two potential paths to that kind of change: the influence of ideas, and campaign finance reform.

This book is my contribution to the battle of ideas. All I can do now is hope that I am not a lone voice in the wilderness and that some of the ideas I have set forth will be shared and echoed by others and can begin to take hold. Having set my ideas forth, all I can really do is step back and wait to see if and how others respond... and monitor and compile responses. But since I am exceedingly curious to know, perhaps here again, you might take the time to visit www.2PctSolution.com, and provide some feedback? If you fill out a survey form or provide some commentary response, I'll make an effort to accumulate and distribute the responses.

Which brings me back to my final topic: campaign finance reform. As with tax reform, I believe the challenge of campaign finance reform screams out for specific and active response.

Unfortunately, as noted back on page 143, the Supreme Court recently took a very activist role in asserting that corporations and unions are entitled to use their treasury funds to shout down the voices of individual citizens, a ruling which may have crippled any legislative opportunity to restrict the flow of money into politics. However, since our legislators had shown very limited interest in, or commitment to, implementing fundamental reform, perhaps the ruling is less significant than it might seem. Legislative restraints against money politics were probably always doomed to failure anyway. So perhaps the Court's ruling may prove a blessing in disguise – since it has re-drawn attention to the issue and narrowed the potential options.

In light of the Court's ruling in the *Citizens United* case, I believe there are only two options left to pursue, either:

1. Publicly fund political campaigns in order to make the money irrelevant, or
2. Seek a Constitutional Amendment to redirect the Court.

Addressing option two first, I'm not a constitutional scholar so I can't pretend to understand all the various legal arguments used by the Court in finding its torturous way to this irrationally illogical ruling. What I do know leads me to believe it arises from the fact that since corporations enter into contracts, both with people and among themselves, corporations have come to be treated as having rights of people under contract law. Simple, logical, so far relatively uncontroversial. But the law, acting with willful blindness, has come to extend that interpretation past all logic to conclude that all rights of citizenship now apply to corporations – an interpretation of farcical proportions in response to which a corporation, Murray Hill, Inc. has now filed application to run for a seat in Congress[38].   Bravo for Murray Hill. If the Supreme Court isn't embarrassed by what they've wrought, they should be.

We could, of course, attempt to seek a Constitutional Amendment to provide guidance to the Court. We probably should. It is simply unconscionable to me that the Court has given corporations and unions the power to use the assets of their shareholders or members to advocate political positions with which those shareholders or members may not approve.

But I'm not going to be the one to lead that fight. Perhaps someone else will[39]?

Instead I will refer you back to the suggestions set forth in Chapter 10. We have to facilitate Free Speech relative to political campaigns. Evidently the courts are going to remain aligned against the rights of individuals in favor of a right for big money to shout down individual voices. Absent a constitutional amendment, our only recourse against that appears to be providing an approved forum which will allow politicians to be heard without bowing in fealty to campaign contributors. If we first do that, then the public can apply judgment as to whether they want to support independent, thoughtful candidates, or fund-raising puppets.

Is it feasible to think that a political class who has grown accustomed to feeding at the trough of big money contributors would voluntarily initiate a change in approach? I think some would. I think the best would.

Given some public support and encouragement, I think the best of our public servants would gladly turn their backs on the rubber-chicken fundraising circuit and re-direct their time and attention more fully toward the challenges of government. I also think that if we could minimize fund-raising demands upon our candidates we might begin to attract a broader assortment and higher quality of citizen to public office. I think we need to offer them that support and encouragement. Take a look at my Demand petition drafted on page 205 and if you agree with what it says, sign on to www.2PctSolution.com and add your voice to the call.

Then, if our Representatives refuse to listen?.... We ought to vote them out of office.

Anyone who either shares or disputes these views is welcome to visit www.2PctSolution.com and participate in the dialogue.

Once again, thank you for joining me as I have exercised what I perceive to be my civic duty. Hopefully I'm not alone in my perspectives. But even if I am, I

---

[38]See http://www.murrayhillweb.com/pr-012510.html
[39] If you do, please contact me, I will gladly sign your petition.

urge you to take steps to exercise your own civic duty by providing guidance to our governing class through both your opinion and your vote.

S. Douglas Hopkins
Sparta, NJ
June 2010

*The following **Petitions for Action** are addressed to the **U.S. Congress and White House** and are posted on line at www.2pctsolution. com. Please review them with care. If you share the sentiments expressed, I urge you to please log on, add your name to the petitions, and thereby **Add Your Voice** to my **Call for Action**.*

I SUPPORT THE 2% SOLUTION

I support repeal of all investment income and estate and inheritance taxes and demand that they be replaced by an Annual Tax on Net Assets of no more than 2%.

I support abolition of the complex and variable exclusions, deductions, credits and multiple tax rate schedules which result in capriciously unequal tax assessments against earned income.

I assert that unless Social Security and Medicare Contributions are held in Trust and backed by tangible investment assets (as opposed to the existing unfunded and unsecured promises of the Federal Government) such taxes constitute nothing more than general tax revenues, and the government's allegations otherwise constitute a fraud against the American people. I allege there is no Trust Fund.

I support abandoning the fiction of separate Social Security/Medicare Taxes and establishment of a simple two-tier income tax schedule with a Tier One Rate of 15% and Second Tier step-up not to exceed 30% in aggregate. I demand that Congress acknowledge that Social Security/Medicare Benefits are being funded and shall continue to be funded from general tax revenues.

I demand Congress take immediate steps to balance the budget in reliance upon the combined available revenues from the aforementioned 2% Asset Tax and Two-Tier Income Tax.

I demand Congress take immediate steps to reduce the National Debt.

I demand that our Government stop expanding unfunded and unsustainable entitlements. I demand that our Government reconcile its tax policies with its promised disbursements.

I demand that our Federal Government start acting in a fiscally responsible manner.

I AM INTRIGUED BY THE 2% SOLUTION

I demand that our Federal Government start acting in a fiscally responsible manner.

I believe that it is wrong that the working class currently bears a higher effective overall tax burden (combined Federal Income Tax and Employment Taxes) on wages and salaries than is assessed against income earned by their more affluent neighbors.

I assert that unless Social Security and Medicare Contributions are held in Trust and backed by tangible investment assets (as opposed to the existing unfunded and unsecured promises of the Federal Government) such taxes constitute nothing more than general tax revenues, and the government's allegations otherwise constitute a fraud against the American people. I allege there is no Trust Fund.

I believe that class warfare based on intellectually dishonest misrepresentations about tax policy is wrong.

I am intensely worried about the impact that existing systemic deficits will have upon our nation and our children's future.

I am intrigued by the suggestion that a 2% tax on Net Assets could expand the revenue base of the Federal Government and assist in stabilizing budget deficits without discouraging investment or growth.

I demand Congress impanel a commission to investigate and evaluate the prospects and implications of replacing existing investment income taxes with an Asset Tax Assessment and provide open public hearings as to its findings and recommendations.

I DEMAND
CAMPAIGN FINANCE REFORM

I believe that the design of America's Democracy requires the service of Citizen Representatives, but existing campaign finance requirements obstruct the ability for its best citizens to serve.

I believe that the existing campaign finance requirements placed on political candidates are so prohibitive that they are corroding the quality of our government.

I believe that the obligation of our Elected Representatives is to exercise their virtue, wisdom and judgment and serve the broad interests of the entire populace – not the narrow interests of their campaign contributors or electoral majority. However, I believe that the prohibitive costs of mounting an effective campaign require our candidates to sell their votes and opinions to their campaign contributors. I believe the perpetual fund-raising process is an obstacle to the practice of good governance.

Efforts to limit the influence of big-money donors have been effectively blocked by self-interested politicians and arguments that the right to spend obscene sums of money is protected as "free speech".

However, I believe the unfettered flow of money into political campaigns has turned the right of free speech into the right to buy control of the conversation.

I demand Congress provide public money and a public forum for legitimate candidates in order to return the right of Free Speech to the Individual and remove the taint of money which now discolors every political campaign.

Appendix I
Tax Policy Center – Distribution of Tax Filers with Zero or negative Tax Liability

Percentage of Tax Units with Zero or Negative Individual Income Tax Liability
By Filing Status and Cash Income Level, Current Law, 2009[a]

Cash Income (2009 dollars)[b]	Tax Filing Status				Elderly Tax Units	Tax Units with Children	All Tax Units
	Single	Married Filing Jointly	Head of Household	Married Filing Separately			
Under $10,000	99.9	100.0	99.7	97.3	100.0	99.9	99.8
$10,000-$20,000	74.3	99.9	99.3	57.9	89.5	99.8	83.6
$20,000-$30,000	36.7	90.2	92.3	26.2	76.5	98.9	61.8
$30,000-$40,000	16.0	79.8	77.9	13.7	61.4	89.3	47.5
$40,000-$50,000	7.4	71.7	45.1	17.1	48.2	68.3	35.7
$50,000-$75,000	5.0	34.2	21.2	4.9	22.5	40.9	21.5
$75,000-$100,000	3.6	11.3	8.2	8.8	8.1	15.1	9.2
$100,000-$200,000	4.0	3.4	2.1	9.3	4.9	4.0	3.5
$200,000-$500,000	3.0	1.8	2.5	4.8	3.9	1.6	2.0
$500,000-$1,000,000	2.6	1.8	5.3	0.0	1.6	2.1	2.0
Over $1,000,000	2.0	1.5	0.0	0.0	1.1	1.3	1.5
All	46.7	38.1	71.9	25.8	55.3	54.1	46.9

Source: Urban-Brookings Tax Policy Center Microsimulation Model (version 0509-2).
[a]Calendar year. Includes both filing and nonfiling units but excludes those that are dependents of other tax units.
[b]Tax units with negative cash income are excluded from the lowest income class but are included in the totals. For a description of cash income, see http://www.taxpolicycenter.org/TaxModel/income.cfm

Tax Policy Center
Urban Institute and Brookings Institution

The Tax Policy Center, a joint venture of the Urban Institute and the Brookings Institution, provides independent, timely, and accessible analysis of current and emerging tax policy issues for the public, journalists, policymakers, and academic researchers. For more tax facts, see http://www.taxpolicycenter.org/taxfacts.

TAX NOTES, June 29, 2009

1583

Appendix II
IRS Collections – Net of Refunds and Aggregate Federal State and Local Tax Burden
2007 / 2008 / 2009

United States
Internal Revenue Collections - Net of Refunds
By Source / Type of Tax (IRS.gov/taxstats Table 1)
$Billions

	Fiscal Year 2007		Fiscal Year 2008		Fiscal Year 2009	
Individual Income Tax	$1,118	46.6%	$1,060	45.8%	$843	44.2%
Employment Taxes	838	35.0%	878	37.9%	855	44.8%
Corporation Income Tax	369	15.4%	301	13.0%	130	6.8%
Excise Taxes	46	1.9%	49	2.1%	45	2.4%
Estate Taxes	24	1.0%	26	1.1%	20	1.1%
Estate & Trust Income Tax					12	0.6%
Gift Taxes	2	0.1%	3	0.1%	3	0.2%
Total Net Revenues	**$2,396**	**100.0%**	**$2,316**	**100.0%**	**$1,908**	**100.0%**

Aggregate National Tax Burden **Federal State and Local** **FY2009** **$Billion**				
	Federal	**State & Loocal**	**Combined**	**Percent of Total**
Individual Income Tax	$843	$251	$1,094	34.8%
Employment taxes	855	-	855	27.2%
Corporation Net Income Tax	130	48	178	5.7%
Property taxes		443	443	14.1%
General Sales & Gross Receipts		283	283	9.0%
Motor Fuels		37	37	1.2%
Tobacco Products		17	17	0.5%
Alcoholic Beverages		6	6	0.2%
Motor Vehicle & Oper Licenses		23	23	0.7%
All Other	80	127	207	6.6%
Total	**$1,908**	**$1,234**	**$3,142**	**100%**
Percent of Total	**61%**	**39%**	**100%**	
Estim GDP			$14,200	
Tax as % of GDP	13.4%	8.7%	22.1%	
Aggreg. Adjusted Gross Income (2007)			$8,000	
Tax as % of 2007 AGI	**23.9%**	**15.4%**	**39.3%**	

Aggregate National Tax Burden Federal State and Local FY2008 $Billion				
	Federal	**State & Loocal**	**Combined**	**Percent of Total**
Individual Income Tax	$1,118	$292	$1,410	38.4%
Employment taxes	838	-	838	22.8%
Corporation Net Income Tax	369	60	428	11.7%
Property taxes		403	403	11.0%
General Sales & Gross Receipts		305	305	8.3%
Motor Fuels		39	39	1.1%
Tobacco Products		16	16	0.4%
Alcoholic Beverages		6	6	0.2%
Motor Vehicle & Oper Licenses		23	23	0.6%
All Other	72	132	204	5.6%
Total	**$2,396**	**$1,276**	**$3,672**	**100%**
Percent of Total	61%	39%	100%	
Estim GDP			$14,000	
Tax as % of GDP	17.1%	9.1%	26.2%	
Aggreg. Adjusted Gross Income (2007)			$8,000	
Tax as % of 2007 AGI	**30.0%**	**16.0%**	**45.9%**	

Aggregate National Tax Burden Federal State and Local FY2007 $Billion				
	Federal	State & Loocal	Combined	Percent of Total
Individual Income Tax	$1,060	303	$1,363	37.6%
Employment taxes	878	-	878	24.2%
Corporation Net Income Tax	301	52	353	9.7%
Property taxes		420	420	11.6%
General Sales & Gross Receipts		306	306	8.5%
Motor Fuels		38	38	1.0%
Tobacco Products		17	17	0.5%
Alcoholic Beverages		6	6	0.2%
Motor Vehicle & Oper Licenses		23	23	0.6%
All Other	77	143	220	6.1%
Total	$2,316	$1,308	$3,624	100%
Percent of Total	61%	39%	100%	
Estim GDP			$14,400	
Tax as % of GDP	16.1%	9.1%	25.2%	
Aggreg. Adjusted Gross Income (2007)			$8,000	
Tax as % of 2007 AGI	29.0%	16.3%	45.3%	

Appendix III
Previously Unpublished Letter to PBS Newshour:

The following was drafted in a moment of pique on 1/21/10 following a report on PBS NewsHour about the **Supreme Court ruling re: Citizens United**.

Dear Sir/Madam:

Excuse me while I vent.

Typically most of the heartburn and irritation I experience over political and governmental stupidity is generated by elected officials in the executive and legislative branches. Today I am reminded how much mischief and damage can be created by an irresponsible and activist court. I just finished watching a PBS NewsHour discussion of a Supreme Court ruling rolling back restraints Congress had placed in effect to prohibit Corporations and Unions from using Shareholder and Member funds for electoral advocacy.

Relying upon the blatant irrationality of treating Corporations or Unions like citizens entitled to First Amendment protection, the Court has aggressively stepped upon the Legislature's modest attempts to rein in practices which threaten the foundations of our Democratic process.

Focus for just a minute on a quote by Steve Simpson of the Institute for Justice who spoke on your show in support of the ruling, "If speakers are to speak effectively they have to spend money". His point rather deftly defines the problem. If effective speech can only be exercised when it is accompanied by the expenditure of vast sums of money the *average individual's rights of free speech are no more than a figment of our imagination.*

Our legislative institutions have struggled mightily over the issue, weighed the merits, and generated a very narrow and rather modest set of controls which required that political advocacy should remain the province of its citizens. If a Corporation or Union wants to advocate a position it cannot utilize their general treasury funds to do so. They can solicit their shareholders or members to act in such matters (either as individuals or via a PAC), but were prohibited from using general funds to pursue them – a limitation primarily designed to ensure that a Corporation or Union could not speak with the voice of shareholders or members without those shareholders/members express participation. It was a logical and very limited step in a desirable direction.

The Court has overruled them, ordering that if I am a member or shareholder of a Union or Corporation, that organization can use my dues or my fractional interest in the assets of the firm to advocate a policy or candidate without regard to my desires or interests. *Your Union can use your dues to support a candidate or policy that you oppose.* By inserting themselves into this issue, the Court has set back the interests of the Legislature and the People in reining in, in even a modest way, the grotesque arms race of high-dollar campaigns which engage in purchasing control of our political debate and elections. The Court is not protecting free speech; it is dancing upon its grave.

The Court's new ruling is a travesty of tortured logic which actively obstructs legitimate attempts to improve the quality and conduct of political campaigns.

S. Douglas Hopkins
Sparta, NJ
January 21, 2010

Appendix IV
Two Percent Solution
Tax Example (see Chapter 12)
Variable Tax Burdens on Theoretical Investors

	Adam	Bob	Charlie	Dave	Ernesto	Fred	Combined
Invested Assets (Prior YE)	$1,000,000	$1,000,000	$1,000,000	$1,000,000	—	$1,000,000	5,000,000
Investment Gains and Income	45,000	100,000	100,000	150,000		200,000	595,000
Return on Assets	4.5%	10.0%	10.0%	15.0%		20.0%	11.9%
Earned Income	50,000	50,000	50,000	50,000	75,000	200,000	475,000
Investment Income							
- Interest & dividends	45,000						45,000
- Short Term Capital gains		100,000					100,000
- Long Term Capital gains			50,000				50,000
- Unrealized Gains			50,000	150,000		200,000	400,000
Total Income & Appreciation	95,000	150,000	150,000	200,000	75,000	400,000	1,070,000
Currrent Tax Liability							
Earned Income	8,687	8,687	8,687	8,687	14,937	50,406	100,091
Employment Taxes (a)	7,650	7,650	7,650	7,650	11,475	19,043	61,118
Investment Income							—
- Interest & dividends	—						—

	Adam	Bob	Charlie	Dave	Ernesto	Fred	Combined
- Short Term Capital gains		26,296					26,296
- Long Term Capital gains			7,500				7,500
- Unrealized Gains			–				–
Total Taxes	**16,337**	**42,633**	**23,837**	**16,337**	**26,412**	**69,449**	**195,005**
	Adam	Bob	Charlie	Dave	Ernesto	Fred	Combined
% of Taxable Income	17.2%	28.4%	23.8%	32.7%	35.2%	34.7%	29.1%
% of Total Inc & Apprec	**17.2%**	**28.4%**	**15.9%**	**8.2%**	**35.2%**	**17.4%**	**18.2%**
Proposed Tax Liability							
Earned Income (b)	9,000	9,000	9,000	9,000	15,250	46,500	97,750
Employment Taxes - n/a					–		–
2% of Assets (c)	15,000	15,000	16,000	18,000		19,000	103,000
Total Taxes	**24,000**	**24,000**	**25,000**	**27,000**	**15,250**	**65,500**	**200,750**
% of Total Inc & Apprec	**25.3%**	**16.0%**	**16.7%**	**13.5%**	**20.3%**	**16.4%**	**18.8%**
Increase / (Decrease)	7,663	(18,633)	1,163	10,663	(11,162)	(3,949)	5,745

(a) Includes Employer portion

(b) 15% of first $35,000, plus 25% of all subsequent income, no caps (replaces all SS/Med taxes).

(c) Note: for simplicity I have assumed that principal is retained but realized gains might be consumed and thus calculated EOY assets as Open Balance plus Unrealized Assets less $250,000 exclusion

S. Douglas Hopkins is the founder and President of Kestrel Consulting, LLC, a crisis management and turnaround consulting firm which provides advisory and interim management services to a broad and diverse selection of middle-market companies. He is also co-author of *Crafting Solutions for Troubled Businesses: A Disciplined Approach to Diagnosing and Confronting Management Challenges*.

A Citizen's 2% Solution is his self-assigned civics project; wherein, he turns his 25 plus years of experience and his disciplined analytical and diagnostic process toward the political process and the challenge of restoring fiscal sanity to America's budget process.

Mr. Hopkins may be contacted through:

www.kestrelllc.com
or via
author@2pctsolution.com

INDEX

V

Voltaire, 108
voluntary contributions, 106

W

Wall Street Journal, 66, 115
Wall Street's business model, 112–121
    bonuses, 115–116
    IPO proceeds, 114

    market capitalization, 114
    stock trading, 114–115
Warren Buffett's tax returns, 65–66
Wertheimer, Fred, 47
Western mythology, 23
Wilson, Woodrow, 34, 122–123

Z

zero liability filers, 58–61

CPSIA information can be obtained at www.ICGtesting.com
Printed in the USA
BVOW010233080612

292072BV00004B/8/P